SISLEY

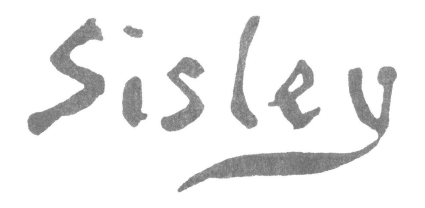

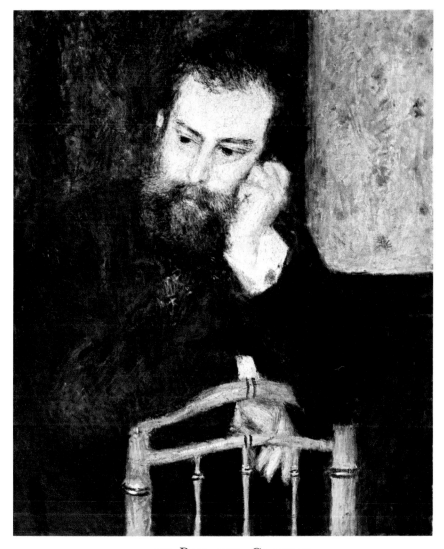

BY RAYMOND COGNIAT

BONFINI PRESS

Title page: PORTRAIT OF ALFRED SISLEY
Oil on canvas, 25 3/4" x 21 3/8" (65,5 x 54,3 cm.)
by Pierre Auguste Renoir, 1875-1876
The Art Institute of Chicago.
Mr. and Mrs. Louis L. Coburn Memorial Collection

Translated from the French by:
ALICE SACHS

Collection published under the direction of:
MADELEINE LEDIVELEC-GLOECKNER

Photographs: Kunst-Dias Blauel, Gauting near Munich - Bulloz, Paris -
Ralph Kleinhempel, Hamburg - IFOT, Grenoble - Lauros-
Giraudon, Paris - Otto E. Nelson, New York - Claude O'Su-
ghrue, Montpellier - Joseph Szaszfai, New Haven, USA.
Plates by Musées Nationaux, Paris - Gerhard Howard, Bern -

PRINTED IN ITALY – INDUSTRIE GRAFICHE CATTANEO S.P.A., BERGAMO – © 1978 BONFINI PRESS CORPORATION, NAEFELS, SWITZERLAND

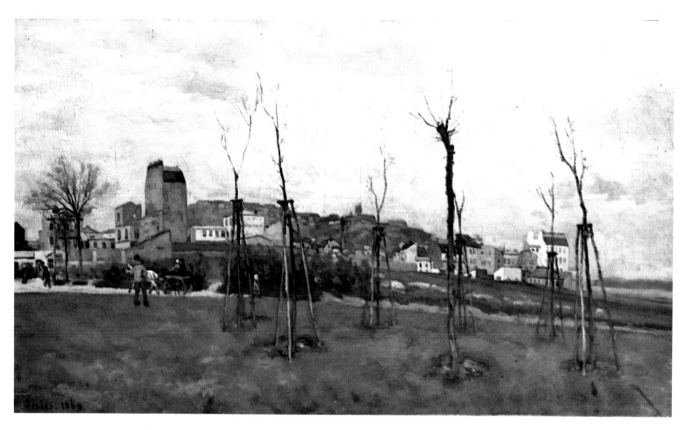

VIEW FROM MONTMARTRE, FROM THE CITY OF FLOWERS AT THE BATIGNOLLES, 1869
Oil on canvas 27$^1/_2$" x 46 (70 x 117 cm.) Grenoble Museum, France

I. - WHY IMPRESSIONISM WAS NEEDED

Neither Sisley's life nor his work can be described as truly colorful or provocative. Both, as they unfolded, were without dramatic incidents if not without difficulties. Yet because his life and work belong to a particular period, they are very significant and can be considered typical of the trends and events of the day, which are cameos of day-to-day existence before becoming History with a capital H. As a start, we must recall anew, if only briefly, the Impressionist adventure in general, in order to put Sisley's life and his contribution to the movement in the proper context. Tradition has it that Impressionism was born in 1874, at the time of the exhibition of « The Cooperative Association of Painters, Sculptors and Engravers » which took place in the studio of the photographer Nadar, 35 boulevard des Capucines.

Louis Leroy, a critic of « Charivari, » (April 25, 1874) found in it an excuse to display his wit, or what he thought of as his wit, by using the word « Impressionists » to designate those « trouble-makers » who proposed to paint their impressions, as it is suggested by the title given by Claude Monet to one of his pictures.

As a matter of fact, the term had been invented several years earlier and had not then applied specifically to this movement. What really matters is the realization that, in essence, Impressionism was something entirely different from a more or less premeditated effort to shock, and that its birth throes were not spontaneously produced by the turmoil of the postwar years. The scandal it caused, or rather the exact time of the scandal, could not have been foreseen; but the organized protests of those who were outraged could be anticipated as the logical outcome of the various demonstrations, most of them more or less disorganized, which for some years had shown a new way of thinking and of painting. Ideas, facts and circumstances all concurred in a general contestation of all aspects of life.

The ideas: first, general ideas on the freedom to which everyone was entitled, freedom both of thought and of action as long as it involved only oneself. Hence the right of each individual to express his own personality; hence the artist's freedom to choose his own subjects and his own techniques.

Likewise, the ideas on the necessity of asserting the vitality of the present — today we would call it creativity — by keeping in constant touch with reality and expanding the stock of knowledge that could be acquired as a result. Hence, for the painter, the need to question nature as closely as possible and thus to reconcile two apparently contradictory elements of his craft: the emphasis on individual sensation and expression and the acceptance of reality.

As to circumstances, when one leaves the realm of theory and enters the world of facts, they are not as susceptible to change as ideas are. From that moment on conflicts are inevitable, for custom and tradition are not easily abandoned even in the face of new directions, and any step forward implies to some extent a denial of the past, which is all the more difficult to accept in view of the fact that every area attempts to find a new structure and to establish a balance between tradition and the continuing revolution which has been taking place for many moons.

The rebellion of artists against traditional molds does not only cause a confrontation, against the style of, broadly speaking, Delacroix and Ingres. Conflicts are also expressed in actual occurrences, such as the first experiment of a Salon without a selection committee, which came about spontaneously (March 15, 1848) during the Revolution of 1848 and which was not followed up because the results were extremely controversial. The « Salon des refusés » (Salon of Rejectees), organized at the instigation of Napoleon III as a protest against the intransigeance of the official selection committee, had a more decisive influence. There were also hostile criticisms of Courbet and Manet and their one-man shows (Courbet's in 1855 and Manet's in 1867) and opposition to them by the Academy (which even extended to Delacroix, who did not become a member of the Institute until 1857), all incidents which helped to exacerbate the belligerence of youth and to add fuel to the fire of their opposition.

Let us recall the birth dates of the men who were to become known as Impressionists:

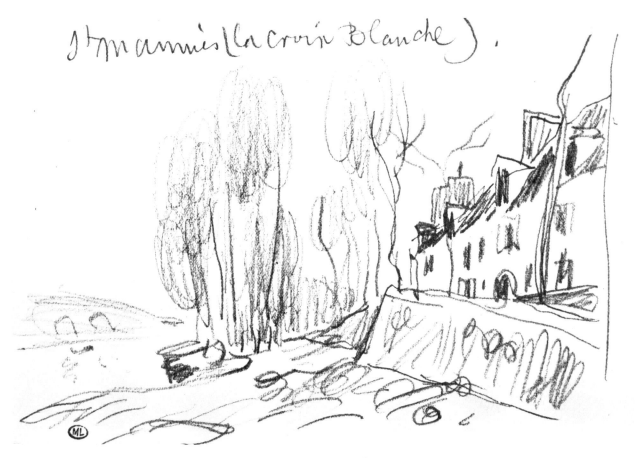

St. Mammès (La Croix Blanche), 1883-1885.
(From the Book of Drawings - Folio 18) 7¹/₂″ x 4³/₄″ (12 x 19 cm.) Louvre Museum, Paris

Pissarro, 1830; Degas, 1834; Cézanne and Sisley, 1839; Monet, 1840; Renoir, 1841. In other words, all of them spent their youthful years in this climate of conflicting claims, which caused them to overlook their differences and make common cause in their mutual desire for independence. All of them, Pissarro more than the others, during their childhood and adolescent years had lived in an atmosphere of social and political tension in which every class of society was eager to see radical changes.

This independence as artists and as individuals involved men who belonged to an economically comfortable stratum of society, as was the case with Sisley, and thus was in the normal order of things at the time, just as the resistance that one and the other experienced was also normal and to be expected.

While we are discussing the events that took place, it is necessary to bear in mind two facts of paramount importance: the first was the invention of photography, which, by reproducing an indisputably accurate image of physical reality, imposed its undeniable truth on artists and gave them the choice of either imitating it, in effect, following the dictates of this mechanical phenomenon, or else going beyond a completely literal realism

7

and achieving a visual result which expressed a more subtle and sensitive verity.

There was another discovery of a material nature, apparently unimportant but far reaching in its consequences: the invention, about 1820, of metal tubes to hold colored paints. This enabled the artist to carry his paints around with him, so that he could paint nature at its source, which had previously been virtually impossible.

Finally the impressionistic technique, with its discrete use of colors, bore a very definite relation to important scientific findings on optics and color made primarily by Chevreul and later by Helmholz and Rood.

Thus a number of facts and events combined so that, in the turmoils of the postwar period of 1870-71, a new conception of art began to emerge, just as new political, social and scientific ideas were flourishing.

The sensation caused by the first Impressionist exhibition in 1874 was repeated in the course of further exhibitions, as well as public auctions, and continued for several years. However, little by little the number of defenders of the Impressionists, both critics and art connoisseurs, increased, and the opposition became less violent. Official circles, notably the Institute, did not waver in their implacable resistance, as illustrated by the vehement protests against the bequest of Caillebotte (who died in 1894). This did not mean that Impressionism had not already won the support of the public, which had been encouraging it for several years; in spite of this, the financial situation of several of the artists involved in the movement, including Sisley, remained precarious.

II. SISLEY'S LIFE
HIS YOUTH (1839-62)

Alfred Sisley was born in Paris on October 30, 1839, in a well-to-do family which, even during this period of social revolution, was able to take over the reins of a profitable business and to take advantage of the expanding opportunities provided by the progress of industry, new financial developments and the establishment of a widespread international exchange. His father, William Sisley, was English (born in Manchester) and was the director of a firm that exported artificial flowers. Their most important clients were in South America. Their business gave them a direct link with a world which was full of life. It enabled them to understand the development of the modern world and to adapt it to their own needs; it also made them especially responsive to any changes, since they worked in the field of fashion, an area particularly dependent on the whim of contemporary society.

Sisley's mother, born Felicia Sell, belonged to an old London family and, raised in an atmosphere of refinement distinguished by its urbanity and sophistication, early became accustomed to genuine good manners, pleasant social gatherings, a good musical training, and in general to a mode of living in an environment of the simple and natural elegance characteristic of high society in England at the time and which ensured her success in France in the era of Romanticism.

In view of these circumstances, it is easy to imagine how serene and untroubled young Sisley's first happy years in Paris must have been. His older brother died at a young age, and two sisters, Emily and France-Aline, were born after him. This halcyon childhood culminated in a first important happening in 1857: when he was eighteen, young Alfred's parents decided to send him to London to perfect his command of the English language by first-hand experience and, at the same time, to prepare himself for a career in business.

The period was favorable to new ideas and independent ventures and offered a vast number of promising opportunities. This general context must be borne in mind in any attempt to comprehend the young man's state of mind as he set off for England. In an interesting concurrence of dates and events, it would seem that the Revolution of 1848, followed by the coup d'état of 1851, heralded the birth of the modern world in France. This was not an easy birth but almost an explosion, heavy with violence and contradictions, with the resistance of the past to completely new conditions of life and work, to new ways of thinking and to new structures that are set up to foster individual initiative.

Consciously or otherwise, the young man could not fail to notice the turbulence of the world. At eighteen, the basic aptitude for a particular career and even more for a particular vocation is already apparent, and indeed has probably been perceptible for several years. Without any definite proof, it may be supposed that, from this time onwards, Sisley felt stirring within him an interest in art and a desire to foster it and, should the occasion arise, to proclaim publicly the attraction it held for his imagination. His biographers tell us that during his stay in London he spent a great deal of his time in museums, was under the spell of Turner, Constable and Bonington and neglected what was supposed to be his initiation into business.

In France, before his departure, and also in England but perhaps to a lesser degree, the artistic cauldron was boiling over with ideas, theories and experiments. It is probable that the youth was well aware of this. The conflict between the partisans of Classicism and the adherents of Romanticism was stirring a permanent rivalry. Courbet's « crude » frankness was considered scandalous, especially after he assembled his important one-man exhibition in 1855 in his « Pavilion of Realism », near the entrance to the International Exhibition. It is altogether likely that Sisley was not unaware of this event, which was widely reported in the press and therefore became a subject of conversation not limited to that sector of the public normally interested in art and esthetics, the echoes of which would still be reverberating down through the following years.

Although we know nothing precise about Sisley's life at this moment, an age so important in the formation of character, we can, by evoking the atmosphere of the period, perceive the germination of the seed that would grow within him shortly thereafter, following his return to France in 1862. Political developments (let us recall the revolutionary ferment of 1848, followed by the coup d'état of Napoleon III in 1851, so important for the French) probably had little effect on him, not only because he was still a child when

Chestnut road at Celle-Saint-Cloud, 1865
Oil on canvas 49$^{1}/_{4}$'' x 80$^{3}/_{4}$'' (50 x 65 cm.)
Museum Ordrupgaard, Copenhagen

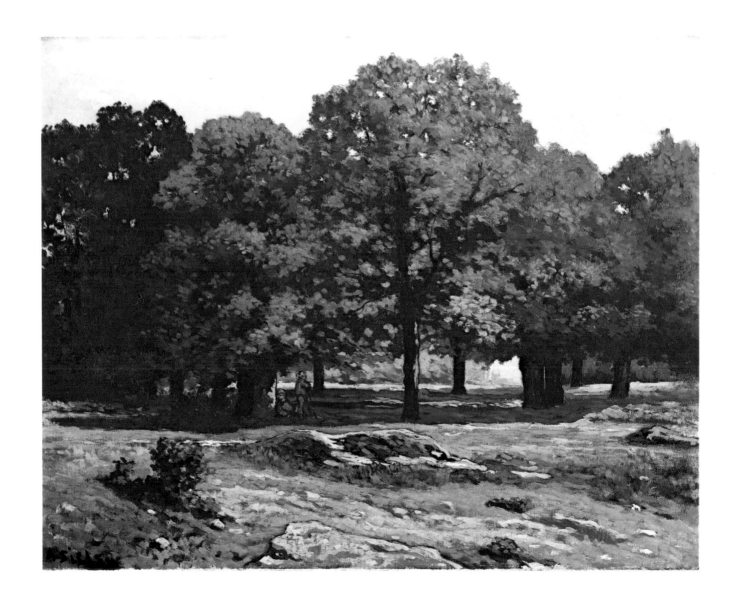

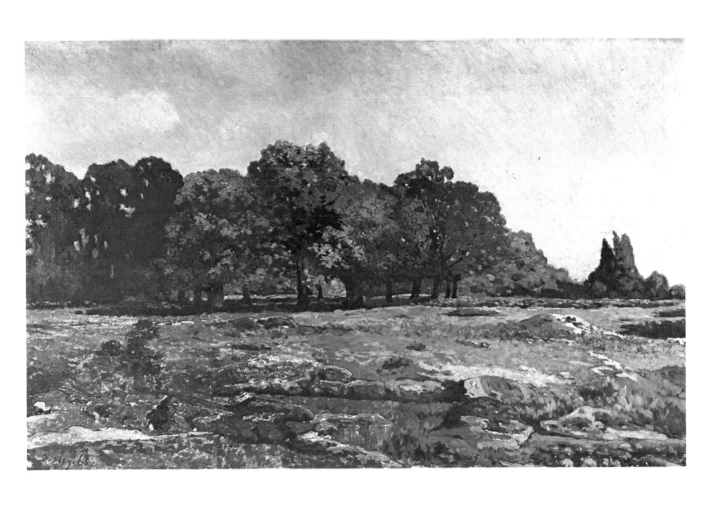

Chestnut road at Celle-Saint-Cloud, 1865
Oil on canvas 19^7/$_8$" x 25^5/$_8$" (125 x 205 cm.)
Museum of the Petit-Palais, Paris

they took place, but also because, given his English origins, they did not seem to concern his social status. Undoubtedly this unawareness was no longer in evidence a few years later when it came to the art revolution, and it was due to the keenness of this conflict that Sisley, by then an adolescent, began to become conscious of his own aspirations.

Raised against a business background, Alfred Sisley was ill prepared to savor the historical-poetical reveries of the romantic and academic painters, and was probably equally unready to accept the too brutal realism of Courbet. His stay in England was bound to strengthen his tendency to concentrate on the harmony of nature, the other face of reality, seen in its pure state without artifice.

Perhaps also the fact that he had been raised in a happy home where there was emphasis on the refined elegance promoted by the world of fashion and that he had seen in his father's business masses of flowers, caused him to develop a certain sense of color harmony as well as a familiarity with the manifold manifestations of nature.

There is another factor which should undoubteddly be taken into account and which up to now we have not mentioned in connection with the things that influenced him during the four years he spent in England. At that time the struggle begun by the creators of Pre-Rephaelism had been waged fiercely for several years. The concepts on which the movement was founded and which guided the artists who practiced them were viewed by contemporaries in an entirely different light from the one we see it in today. What we perceive as being primarily a technique based on symbols (ethereal poetry and mythical evocations) boasted instead that it was a true reproduction of reality and was nourished by it.

In 1853 Ruskin proclaimed: « Pre-Raphaelism has but one principle: to be absolutely and uncompromisingly truthful in all its works. This it achieves by being faithful to nature down to the smallest detail, and letting nature alone inspire its art. All the backgrounds of Pre-Raphaelite landscapes are painted out-of-doors, at the scene, directly from nature, to the last stroke of the brush. All Pre-Raphaelite portraits, however much has gone into their expressions, are faithfully rendered portraits of a living person. Each accessory object, however minor, is painted in the same way ». This movement was at its height in 1857 when Sisley landed in London.

One has to agree that the words just quoted and the underlying principles that lay behind them could equally well have been quoted, twenty years later, to explain the basic concepts of Impressionism. This influence of English painting in gestating the movement, which would in the future take the path which it had blazed, is undoubtedly more important than has been acknowledged and stressed up to now. Sisley perceived its significance and a little later was to pass its principles on to his friends when they reacted against the teaching of the painter Gleyre and decided to work in the open air, adapting, like so many others before them, the theme of reality to justify their innovations.

In this context it is not enough to cite only the names of Turner, Constable and Bonington. A whole wave of English artists, from the end of the eighteenth century to the mid-nineteenth century, had continued to express themselves similarly, particularly through

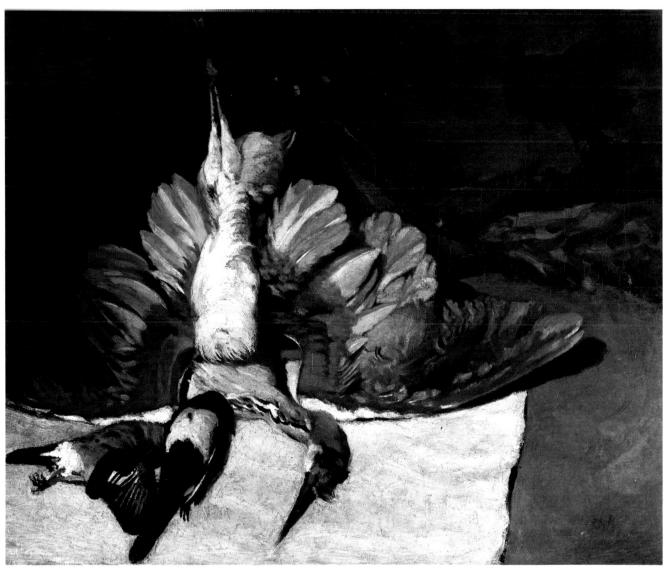

STILL LIFE WITH HERON, 1867
Oil on canvas 31⁷/₈" x 39³/₈" (81 x 100 cm.)
Jeu de Paume Museum, Paris

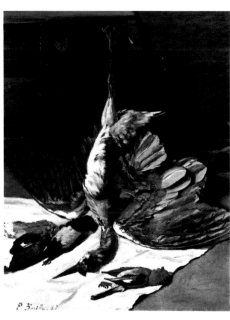

STILL LIFE WITH HERON, 1867
by Fréderic Bazille
Oil on canvas, 39³/₈" x 31" (100 x 79 cm.)
Fabre Museum, Montpellier

BARGES ON CANAL SAINT-MARTIN IN PARIS, 1870
Oil on canvas, 21⁵/₈" x 29¹/₈" (55 x 74 cm.)
Collection: Oskar Reinhardt, Winterthur

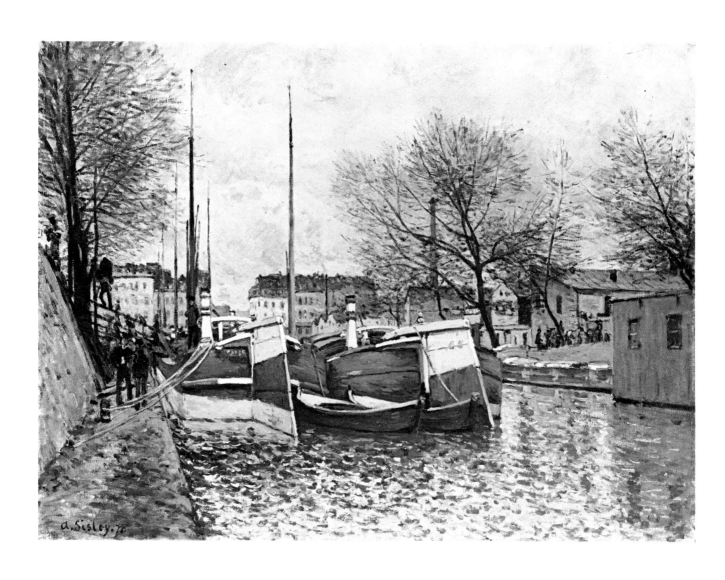

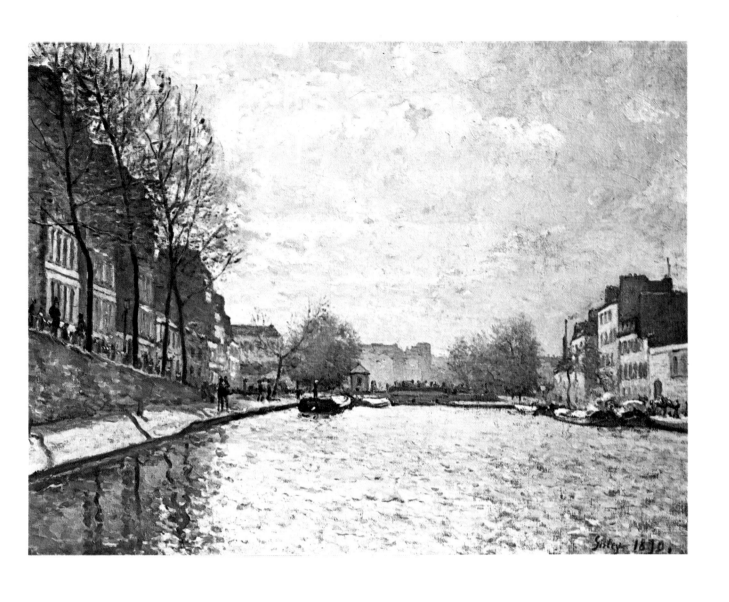

VIEW FROM THE CANAL SAINT-MARTIN, 1870
Oil on canvas, 19$^7/_8$" x 25$^5/_8$" (50 x 65 cm.)
Jeu de Paume Museum, Paris

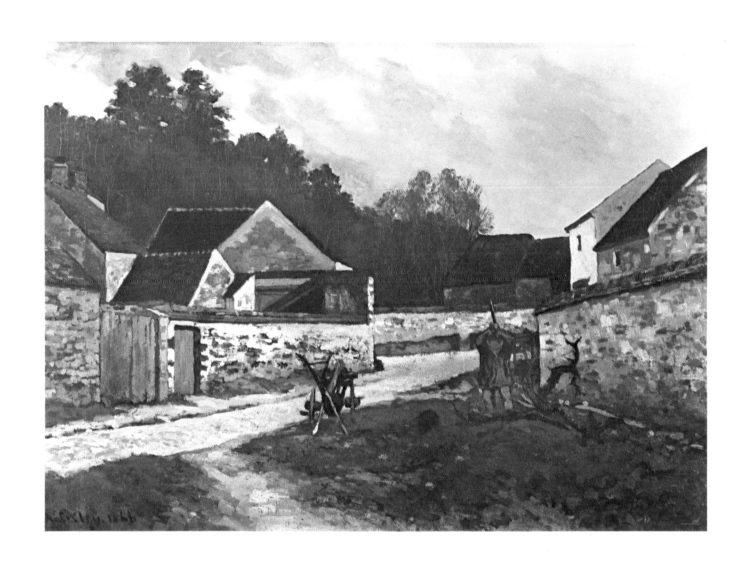

VILLAGE STREET IN MARLOTTE, 1866
Oil on canvas, 25" x 36" (50 x 92 cm.)
Albright- Knox Art Gallery, Buffalo, N.Y.

EARLY SNOW AT LOUVECIENNES, 1870
Oil on canvas, 21^1/$_4$" x 28^3/$_4$ (54 x 73 cm.)
Museum of Fine Arts, Boston, Bequest of
John T. Spaulding

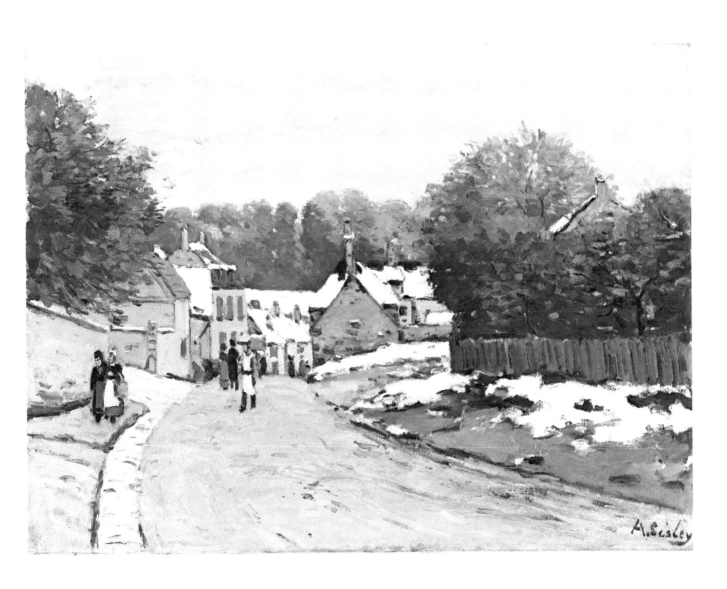

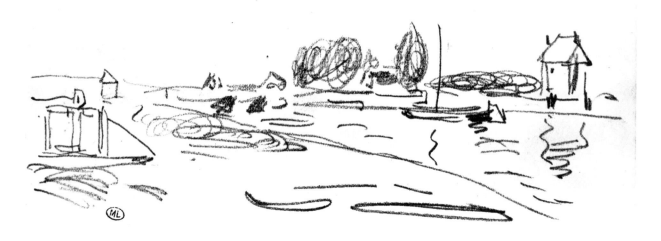

The Canal..., 1883-1885.
(From the Book of Drawings - Folio 43) 4³/₄" x 7¹/₂" (19 x 12 cm.) Louvre Museum, Paris

landscapes. Sisley certainly must have discovered this in London, and welcomed it as a precious heritage to which he was naturally entitled and through which he began to feel that he might find himself and realize his fullest potential.

We have already mentioned the various schools pitted against one another: Romanticism, Academicism and Realism, and the bitterness of their struggle for dominance. It is inconceivable that Sisley was ignorant of this rivalry, but apparently he felt somewhat removed from it. The tradition reached its highest point in the success of *The Romans of the Decadence* by Thomas Couture at the Salon of 1847. Courbet's *Burial at Ornans,* which created a sensation at the 1850 Salon, and Delocroix's « Lyric Tension » certainly provided irrefutable proof that the times were changing but perhaps were not interpreted as such, even if Sisley, who was still too young to be actively involved in the intellectual and artistic ferment of the period, saw them at all. His stay in London, however, must have been a revelation for him, a voyage of self-discovery, at the same time prompting him to appreciate the benefits of the comfortable and seemingly endless security of Queen Victoria's reign. Nonconformist ideas do not necessarily imply a rebellious nature, as is clearly borne out by Sisley's life during the following years.

HIS BEGINNING AS A PAINTER (1862-70)

During the four years Sisley spent in England, his penchant for art became so pronounced that, when he returned to his family in France in the spring of 1862, they had to accept the fact that he was uninterested in business and so permitted him to take painting lessons and to enroll for those given by Gleyre at his academy, which at the time enjoyed an enviable reputation. He entered the academy in October and there made the acquaintance first of Renoir, then of Monet and Bazille, who were also newcomers. It was not long before these neophytes became friends and a group unto themselves.

Charles Gleyre, a painter of Swiss origin, had in 1843 become the successor to Paul Delaroche as the head of this studio. Born in 1806, he arrived in Paris in 1825 and received lessons from Hersent, then from Bonington. He spent a few years in Rome, where he became friendly with his compatriot, Léopold Robert, following which he traveled in the East for three years, returning to Paris in 1837. Thus he belonged to the generation of artists who, following the example of David, practiced a scholarly, formul, orderly Academicism, requiring art to express thought and mental processes, imposing on painting an emphasis

The Loing Canal, 1883-1885.
(From the Book of Drawings - Folio 48) 4³/₄" x 7¹/₂" (19 x 12 cm.) Louvre Museum, Paris

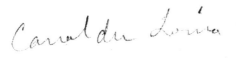

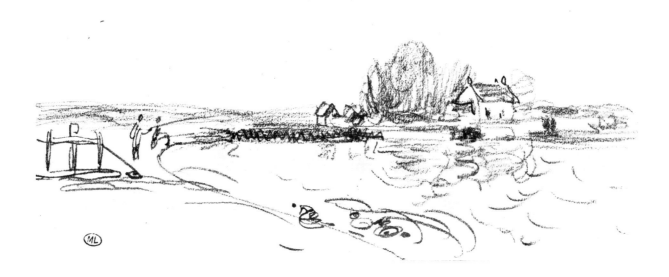

19

THE MACHINE AT MARLY, 1873
Oil on canvas, 18¹/₁₆" x 25⁵/₈" (46 x 65 cm.)
Ny Carlsberg Glyptotek, Copenhagen

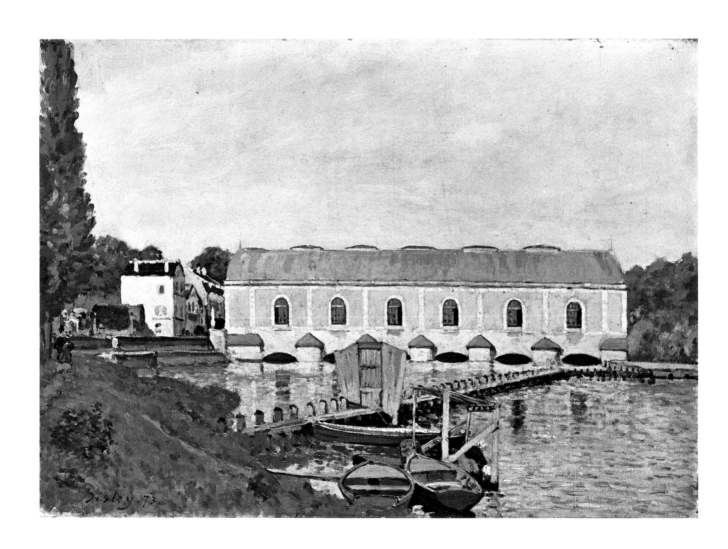

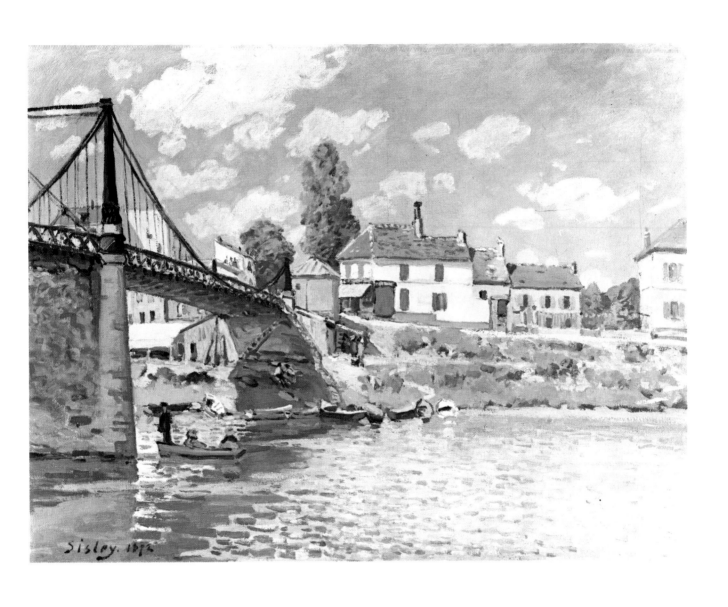

THE BRIDGE AT VILLENEUVE-LA-GARENNE, 1872
Oil on canvas, $19^1/_2$" x $25^3/_4$" (49,5 x 63 cm.)
The Metropolitan Museum of Art Gift of Mr. and Mrs.
Henry Ittleson, Jr.

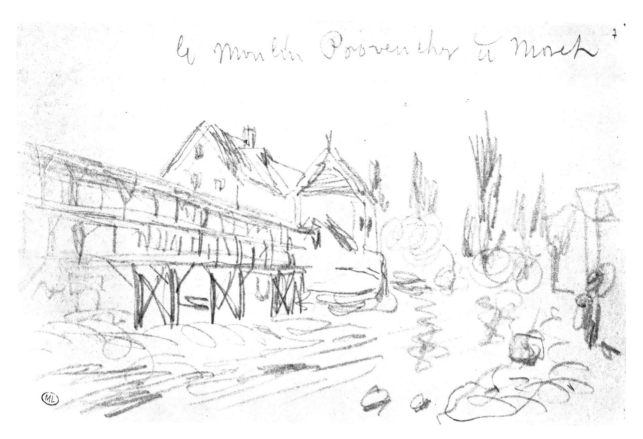

The Mill of Provencher at Moret, 1883-1885.
(From the Book of Drawings - Folio 7) 4³/₄" x 7¹/₂" (19 x 12 cm.) Louvre Museum, Paris

on drawing and composition, and harnessing any instinctive and spontaneous impulses by utilizing rigid scientific and technical controls.

After a difficult period, he achieved an outstanding success in the Salon of 1843. A painter with an historical bent, whose subjects were primarily religious or mythological, he was classified as a romantic, neoclassical artist. He kept his distance from nature and was completely uninterested in landscapes as such. His esthetic vocabulary was derived from social and philosophical ideas which, by the middle of the nineteenth century, had been violently attacked by the various movements through the medium of which young artists were liberating themselves from their elders.

Sisley and his friends, both temperamentally and in a reaction typical of their generation, felt ill at ease at the imposition of strict disciplinarian methods. In this, contrary to what was stated earlier, these young people were completely different from the Pre-Raphaelites both in their ideas and their techniques, as is proved by the balance of the text of Ruskin which we previously quoted: « The habit of painting each detail with the most perfect accuracy finally rendered the Pre-Raphaelites unable to appreciate the merits of artists who, although up to a certain point they claimed to have an identical respect for the truth, nonetheless ordinarily preferred powerfully drawn if hasty strokes to a too meticulous finished work, and the essence of truth to the bald, dry truth. » This summary expresses very well the problem immediately faced by the young students and led them to a solution which was the forerunner of Impressionism.

These two ways of looking at nature and of depicting it on canvas cannot be explained solely by differences in technique. At a more profound level, they are distinguished by two ways of perceiving things and perhaps, at a deeper level, by philosophical and social attitudes which, particularly at that period, were of enormous importance and corresponded to the political movements of the time.

Although there was no doctrinal basis to this, the attempt to impose a particular social order and a strict discipline on the collective lives of French citizens was, as it were, comparable to the discipline, in art, of a technique geared to a literal portrayal of what was defined as reality, a meticulous attention to details which had to be reproduced fully and accurately and a determination not to leave anything to chance. The notion of independence

Courtyard in St. Mammès. Rush Plaiter, 1883-1885.
(From the Book of Drawings - Folio 38) 4³/₄″ x 7¹/₂″ (19 x 12 cm.) Louvre Museum, Paris

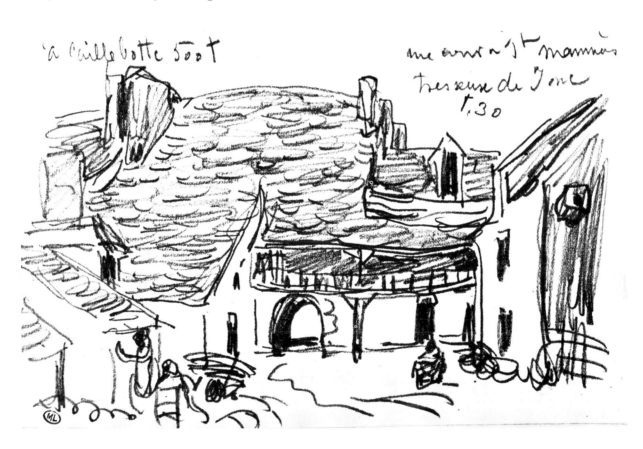

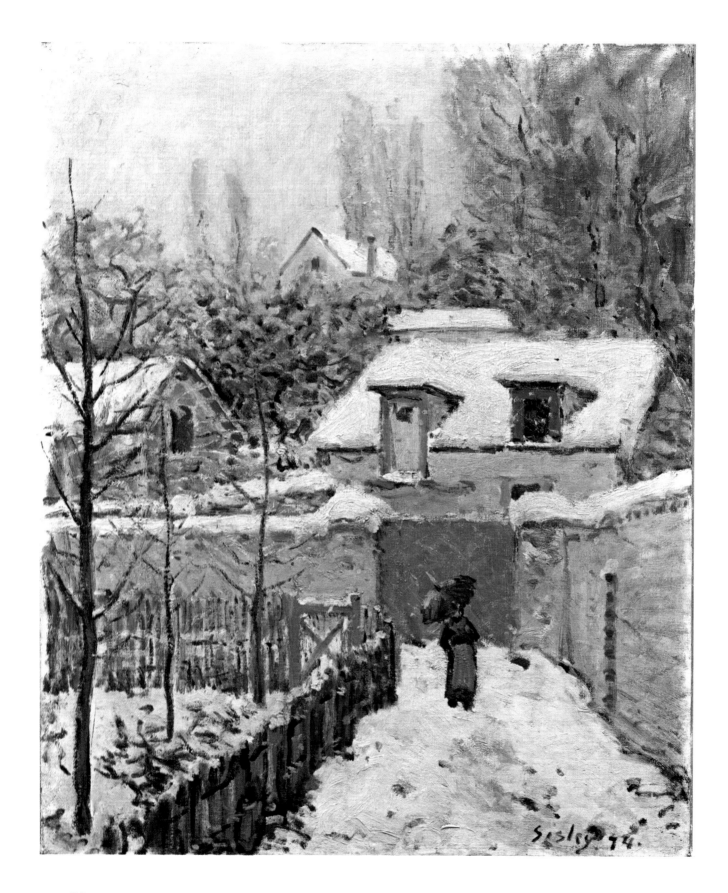

24

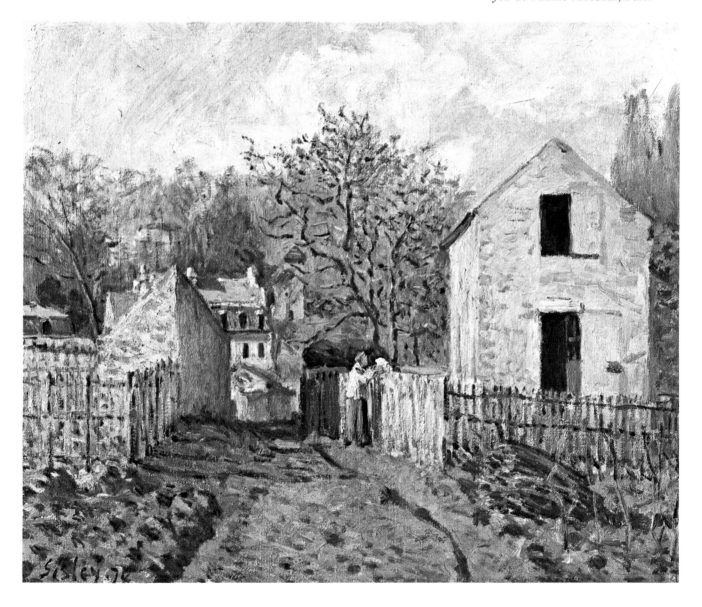

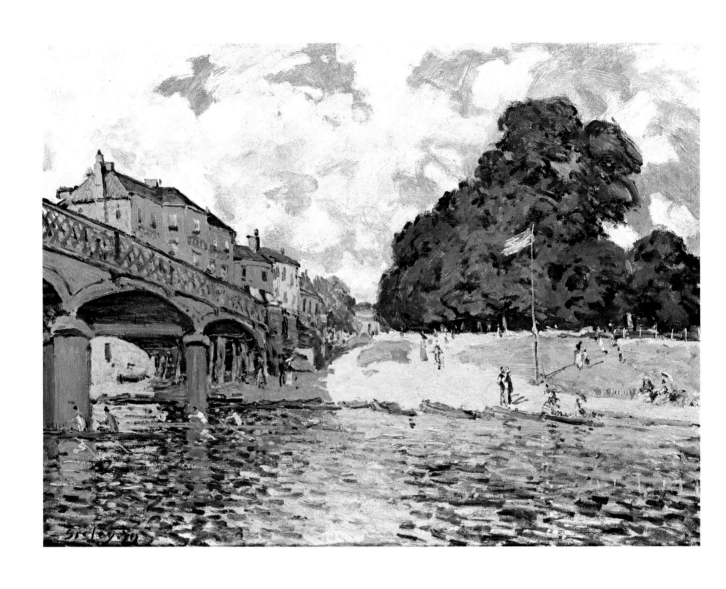

THE BRIDGE AT HAMPTON COURT, 1874
Oil on canvas, 18¹/₁₆" x 23⁵/₈" (46 x 61 cm.)
Wallraf-Richartz Museum and Museum Ludwig, Cologne

26

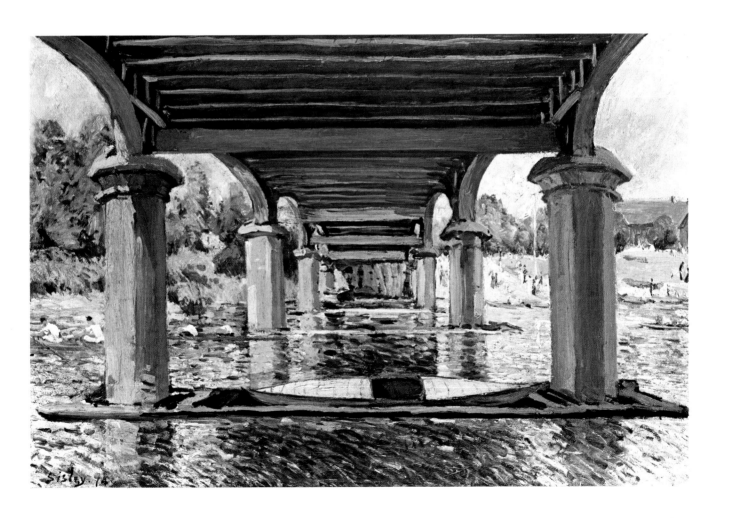

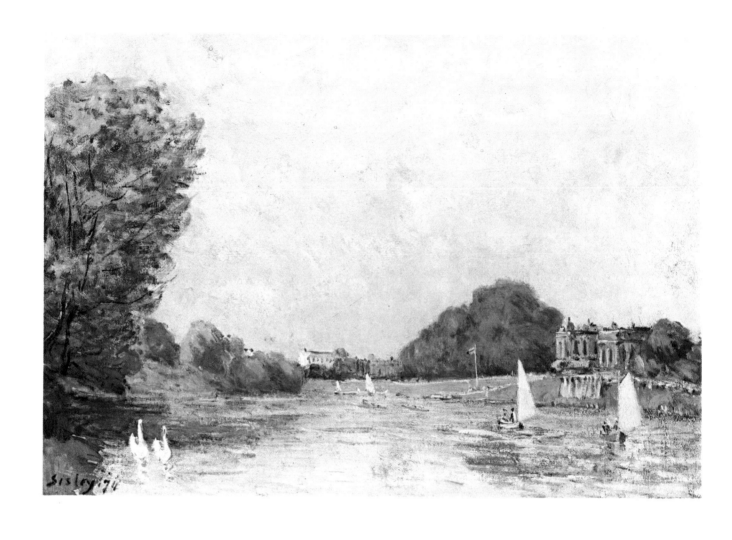

HAMPTON COURT, 1874
Oil on canvas, 15" x 21$^{13}/_{16}$" (38 x 55,4 cm.)
Sterling and Francine Clark Institute, Williamstown, Mass.

tomented by revolution found its counterpart in the artists who displayed a taste for a free interpretation of nature and claimed an inherent right to be outspoken and who let themselves be swayed by the winds of spontaneous and inventive techniques and whatever chance might offer.

The team in Gleyre's studio, instinctively in revolt against the old-fashioned teaching which treated their craft as a closely defined, rigid discipline, were very much in the mainstream of the youth movement of the period and hence refused to accept the politics of repression, imposed in the names of tradition, law and order; that is to say, they rejected the orderly values according to which the subjects of paintings were classified in descending importance, pride of place being reserved for genre paintings, with their symbolism or historical scenes, while landscapes and still lifes were relegated to an inferior place in the artistic firmament. Gleyre's teaching could not be expected to depart from traditional patterns, since this was the tradition which had inspired all of his paintings and brought him whatever success he had achieved.

Neither the spirit nor the substance of his lessons could therefore move the young

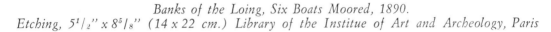

Banks of the Loing, Six Boats Moored, 1890.
Etching, $5^1/_2$" x $8^5/_8$" (14 x 22 cm.) Library of the Institue of Art and Archeology, Paris

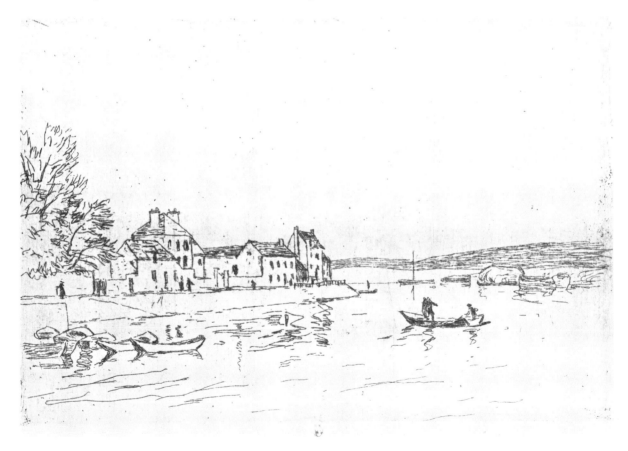

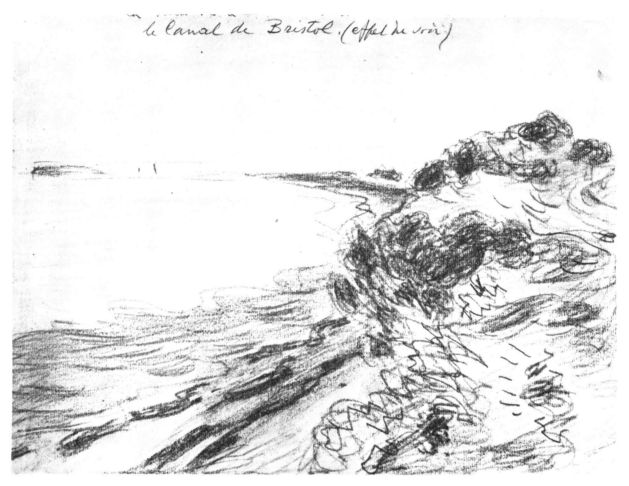

The Bristol Canal. Evening, no date.
Colored pencil on paper, $7^3/8'' \times 10$ (18,8 x 25,3 cm.) Museum of the Petit-Palais, Paris

men for whom, from the beginning, the choice of a career so daring represented the triumph of instinct over reason. How could they submit to what for them would have been a compromise? Very quickly they concluded that they would have to leave the sterile confines of the school if they wanted to seize life's treasure and renounce the symbols of an intellectual art so that they might discover the riches of sensory art. Perhaps one should also recognize in this conflict between the two artistic schools the attempt to defend a craft inspired by individual sensation and a rejection of a mechanical production that turned art into an industry regulated by fixed rules that were both unchanging and impersonal.

It is clear that there were a number of factors that made the group of young painters decide that they could no longer be satisfied by the lessons of their teacher. In March 1863 they began to work in the open air for the first time, in the countryside around Paris. At Easter, they spent a few days in the forest of Fontainebleau, in Chailly-en-Bière, at the White Horse Inn run by Père Paillard. This was the inn about which Bazille wrote to his mother: « We were lodged at the excellent White Horse Inn, where for three francs and seventy-five centimes a day one can have a room and wonderful meals. »

Although they came from backgrounds as diversified as their economic statuses, the four young people seemed to get along perfectly, as demonstrated by the fact that this outing would be repeated time and again during the following years and that their friendship would be reconfirmed. If their social origins and financial resources were dissimilar, their tastes, their ambitions and their ages were practically identical. Sisley, the oldest, was not yet twenty-four; Bazille, the youngest, would soon be twenty-two. They were at that moment in their lives when they had to grapple with their consciences and decide seriously what course to pursue for the rest of their lives.

The four all encouraged one another to break with their pasts and to rid themselves of the illusions and prudent advice given them by their families. Bazille had left Montpellier the year before to come to Paris to study medicine, but also to attend Gleyre's courses. In 1864 he failed to pass his medical examination, and this failure would liberate him from the need to become a doctor and release the latent artist in him. Like Sisley, he could count on financial aid from his parents, which permitted him to try his luck with the assurance of at least a modicum of economic security.

Renoir, a modest craftsman without any income other than that engendered by his work, for a long time persevered in painting religious themes on shades for missionaries, a chore that enabled him to put aside a small nest egg, thanks to which he was finally able to give up the daily routine of earning a livelihood and to take painting lessons. Those of Gleyre were a last resort for someone with Renoir's temperament and sparkling vitality.

Monet had just been discharged from the army and, after spending the summer of 1862 in Le Havre in the company of Boudin and Jongkind, also was on the brink of making a definite decision about his future.

In fact, it was at that moment that Impressionism was actually born, in that springtime of 1863, when four young men united to affirm the mutual pleasure they took in painting, not according to the rules promulgated by any school, but under the inspiration of nature.

Without any earth-shaking announcement, they had just taken a decisive step in the battle against hard-and-fast rules. And as if to encourage them for having made their provocative, even revolutionary decision, on May 15, 1863, the « Salon des refusés » (Salon of Rejectees) opened. It had been created at the instigation of Napoleon III to display the works turned down for the official Salon by an exceptionally severe selection committee. Manet's *Picnic* caused a sensation as much because of its theme as because of the way in which he had handled it. The struggle had begun for painting with a light palette. The battle for spontaneous and unacademic painting had been waged and won by Delacroix, who had just died on August 13 and for whom an important retrospective exhibition was to be held the following year, in 1864, to remind the public of his accomplishments.

The road that lay before the young men seemed open, but they were still cautious about advancing too far along it; for however certain they were that they wanted to have nothing to do with the outdated esthetic modes dear to their elders, they were not yet sure what form their efforts should take or where their impulses might lead them. The sensation caused by Delacroix and, much more recently, Manet, offered them some clues, suggested the general direction to be taken in order to build on the far less radical and more cautious, but no less characteristic, experiments of the Barbizon painters. The idea of enriching art by the direct observation of nature was in the air. John Rewald, in his excellent study of Impressionism, quotes a passage which is almost a prophecy: « In 1865 », he says, « a critic called Daubigny "the leader of the school of Impression," and in 1863 Castagnary wrote of Jongkind: "With him everything depends on impression". »

What do we know about the work of these future Impressionists except the result of their first contacts with the forest of Fontainebleau? Very little, in fact. We do not know any paintings by Sisley prior to the two landscapes of Celle-Saint-Cloud (one of them, in the Petit-Palais collection, is dated 1865 and thus provides us with accurate knowledge as to the year of his debut). (see pp. 10, 11). Their motif is the same and shows that Sisley, even at this early date, had abandonned any desire to vary his subjects but, on the contrary, preferred to return over and over again to those already familiar to him. Speculation about the nature of his previous experiments might be justified, since we know nothing about

Cabins on the Beach, 1897.
Colored pencil on paper, 6¹/₈″ x 9⁷/₈″ (15,5 x 25 cm.) Museum of the Petit-Palais, Paris

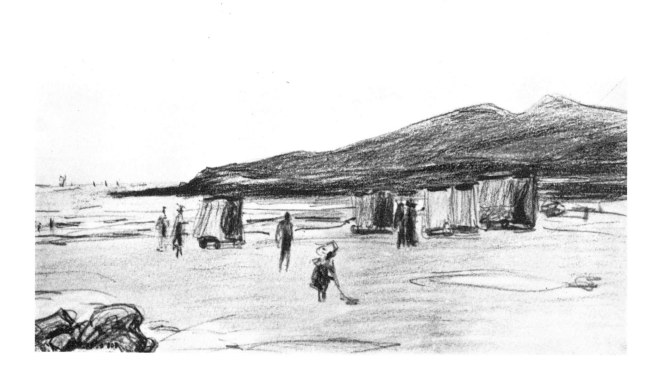

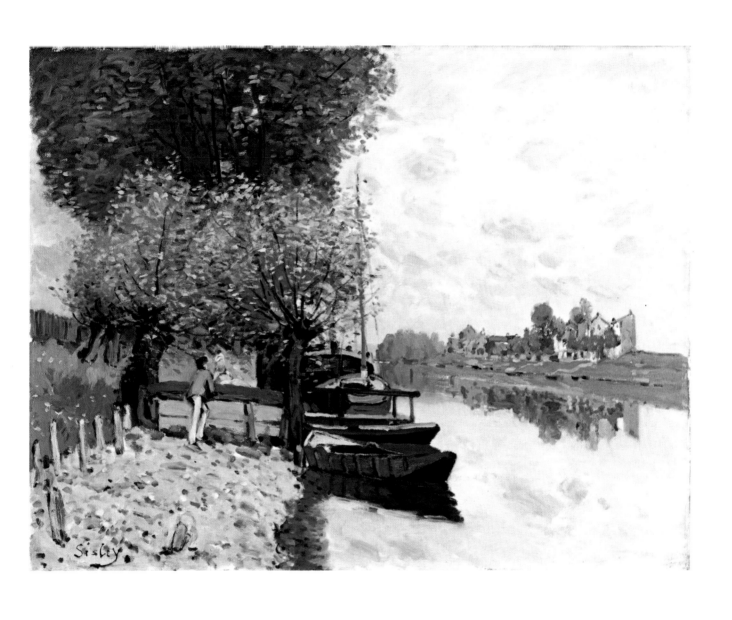

THE SEINE AT BOUGIVAL, 1872
Oil on canvas, 20" x 25" (50,8 x 63,5 cm.)
Yale University Art Gallery,
Gift of Henry Johnson Fisher

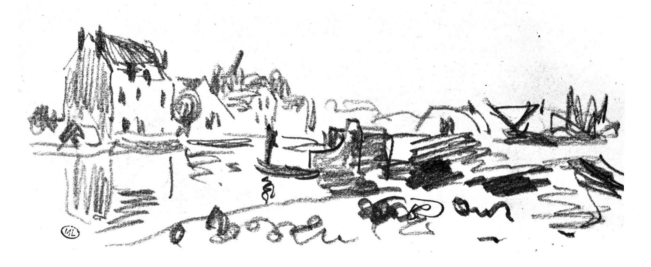

The Loing at St. Mammès, 1883-1885.
(From the Book of Drawings - Folio 3) $4^3/_4$" x $7^1/_2$" (19 x 12 cm.) Louvre Museum, Paris

them, but it is probable that the views of the forest of Fontainebleau of 1863 were, like the landscapes of 1865, strongly influenced by Corot, as well as the two paintings of 1866 depicting a street in the village of Marlotte, which were accepted by the Salon of the same year (see p. 16).

By studying these four examples, we can already discern certain characteristics that were to be typical of his entire output, such as the marked difference between his method of depicting trees and houses. He uses a supple line for the forms and substance of trees but a much stronger line and firmer touch for houses.

All the evidence suggests that these paintings are not the work of a beginner, and while Sisley has not yet freed himself completely from outside influences, he was already showing signs of enormous skill and even of technical mastery, as well as maturity in his observation of nature. Yet he does not display any aggressive hostility towards the world of officialdom; in fact, the painter proved this by submitting his works in 1866 to the Salon, even though he had been among those who signed a document protesting against some proposed new rules for the Ecole des Beaux-Arts.

34

The two paintings accepted by the Salon of 1866 depict the village of Marlotte in the forest of Fontainebleau, near Barbizon, where Sisley had settled in April of the previous year with Renoir, in the inn run by Mère Anthony, where Monet and Pissarro were soon to join them. At Celle-Saint-Cloud a few weeks later (in May, according to François Daulte) he painted the two landscapes of 1865 mentioned above. The alley of chestnut trees was used as a subject twice, first in its entirety, then more closely so that its details could be better observed, as if he were trying to invoke something of the spirit of the Barbizon painters, for whom each tree frequently had a distinct personality, like a living being (this was especially true of Théodore Rousseau).

In July 1865, still accompanied by Renoir, Sisley sailed down the Seine and had the boat towed to Rouen before going on to Le Havre to attend the regatta. It must have been a joyous escapade, for Sisley, like Renoir, had the reputation of being very good company and of relieving by his good humor any anxiety caused by the uncertainties of their budding careers.

These were not months spent in idleness, for painting already occupied too important a place in both of their lives to be a mere pastime to fill their leisure hours. Yet there remains nothing of the work which must have been done the following year except for the two canvases already mentioned.

The year 1866 was notable for another happy event: the artist's marriage, that summer, to Marie-Eugénie Lescouezec, a Parisian originally from Toul, by whom he was to have two children, Pierre and Jeanne.

One of the first of Sisley's still lifes can be dated with a fair degree of certainty, since it depicts exactly the same subject as the one treated in a picture by Bazille which bears the legible date of 1867. It is interesting to compare these paintings. Sisley's personal style appears less fully developed than that of Bazille, whose drawing is sharper and whose use of color more definite. Sisley is less assertive and firm, but he is obviously no longer a mere novice (see p. 13).

It was probably around that time that he painted some still lifes, including a fish and, more notably, a pheasant, the latter suggesting that he was already well on the way to developing a more personal technique.

The friendship of the young artists and the long periods spent together undoubtedly influenced their art and led them to make similar statements on the nature of freedom, to the point where all four (Sisley, Renoir, Bazille and Pissarro) in that same year 1867 had their works rejected by the selection committee of the Salon. They then signed a petition demanding in vain that once again a « Salon des refusés » (Salon of Rejectees) be held.

After a brief stay at Honfleur in July, Sisley returned to Chailly to join Renoir. Despite the indifference or the prejudices of art collectors and dealers, notwithstanding the difficulties Daubigny faced every year as he tried to overcome the hostility of the selection committee, despite their extremely modest and sometimes precarious financial situation — except in the case of Sisley and Bazille — the young men appeared to be living in an atmosphere generally favorable to the flowering of their artistic talents, and their art

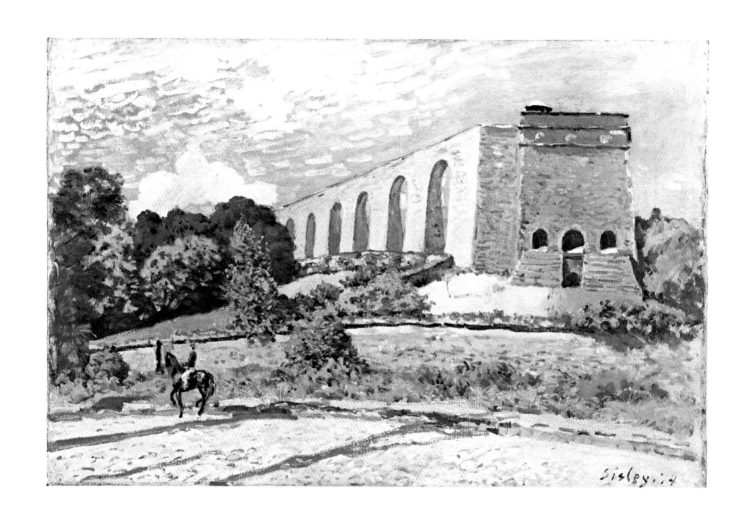

THE AQUEDUC AT PORT-MARLY, 1874
Oil on canvas, 21³/₈" x 32" (54,3 x 81,3 cm.)
The Toledo Museum of Art, Toledo, Ohio,
Gift of Edward Drummond Libbey

already bore the imprint of the serenity which, even in the face of adversity and up to the very last paintings, was destined to impart a homogeneity of feelings to the works of the Impressionists.

A dual portrait of Sisley and his wife by Renoir, done during their stay at Chailly-en-Bière in the spring of 1868, is significant in this context because it expresses so well the tenderness that united the young couple, their graciousness and also the affection Renoir felt for them and his genuine desire to put on canvas the emotion which their agreeable elegance, as seen in their gestures as well as in their clothes, inspired in him.

Apart from their meetings in the outskirts of Paris or Fontainebleau, the young painters congregated in Paris at the Café Guerbois, 9 or 11 Grande rue des Batignolles (which after 1868 became the avenue de Clichy), where they met through Manet a group of writers and critics, most of whom were already or were soon to become their defenders. All of them engaged in discussions on the virtues of Realism and its successor, Naturalism: Philippe Burty, Duranty, Emile Zola, Duret, Armand Silvestre and Paul Alexis. Other painters of their generation also formed part of the circle, some students at the academy Suisse (frequented by Cézanne, Pissarro, Guillaumin) and others such as Bracquemond, Marcellin Desboutin and Fantin-Latour. Among the other patrons of the same café were Constantin Guys, Alfred Stevens and occasionally the photographers Nadar and Carjat.

Sisley came to these gatherings as a neighbor, for ever since his return from England he had shown a partiality for the new quarter of the Plaine Monceau and its surroundings, which had recently become a part of the city of Paris (in 1860) and now formed the 17th « arrondissement. » He lived in turn at 31 avenue de Neuilly, near Porte Maillot, in 1864; then in 1866 at 15 rue Moncey; still later, at the beginning of 1868, at 9 rue de la Paix, which that same year was renamed rue de la Condamine; and finally at 27 Cité des Fleurs, an oasis of small houses with their own gardens, which started at 154 avenue de Clichy.

In this Cité des Fleurs he painted in 1869 a view of Montmartre (see p. 5) which is one of the most important works of the period and testifies to the still rustic nature of the new quarter. Sisley continued to paint very little, for this work is the only one dated 1869. However, it is probable that most of the paintings he had produced since his debut in 1862 were either lost or destroyed, for as has already been said, it does not seem possible, even if we consider only what he must have produced from the time of his first stay at Marlotte in 1865, that his work consisted solely of eight landscapes and four still lifes.

After 1870, there begins a period of more fruitful creative production. There were six landscapes, two of them views of the Canal Saint-Martin, which were to be accepted by the Salon of the same year. These two works represent an important step forward for the artist because, for the first time, he uses lighter colors than hitherto and short, separate strokes to suggest the reflection of light on the water, a technique which was to become one of the hallmarks of Impressionism (see pp. 14, 15).

In addition, the choice of themes is new. For the first time, we have landscapes in

PORT-MARLY BEFORE THE FLOODS, 1876
Oil on canvas, 15" x 21³/₄" (38 x 55 cm.)
Private collection

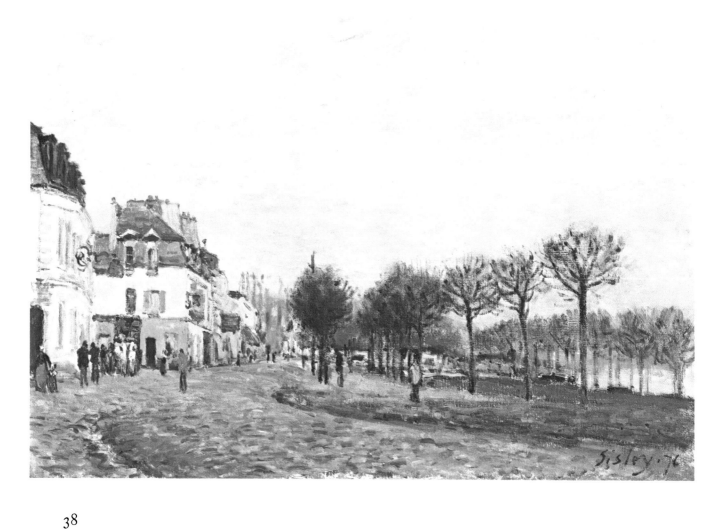

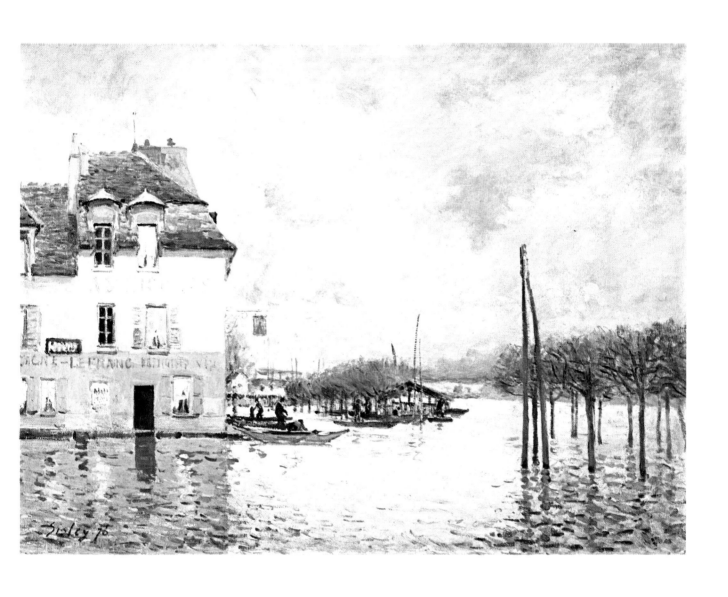

FLOODS AT PORT-MARLY, 1876
Oil on canvas, 23¹/₂" x 31¹/₈" (60 x 80 cm.)
Jeu de Paume Museum, Paris

39

which water occupies a very important place in relation to the other elements. It is also the first time the artist, in another canvas, paints a street in Louveciennes, a street moreover which is covered with snow, another new departure which was to be repeated frequently in the future (see p. 17).

Thus it would seem that 1870 can be considered a starting point, a sample, as it were, of what was to be developed and shown later. It is all the more significant in the Renoir, Monet and Pissarro, all of whom had a recent past in which their talents became more apparent, and in which they had produced a greater number of works and even some large paintings with human figures, had, even before Sisley, discovered the light along the banks of the Seine, from Argenteuil to Bougival, around Louveciennes and Marly. Thus, without realizing it, they had inaugurated the first of a long series of landscapes which were to give the works of the Impressionists a remarkable esthetic unity.

Landscape, no date.
Colored pencil on paper, 6¹/₄" x 9⁵/₈" (16 x 24,5 cm.) Museum of the Petit-Palais, Paris

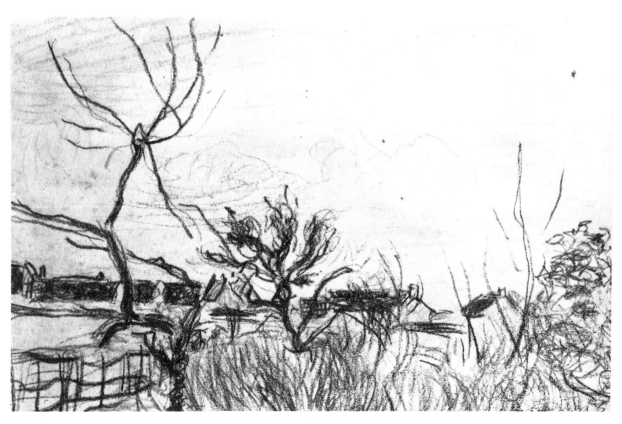

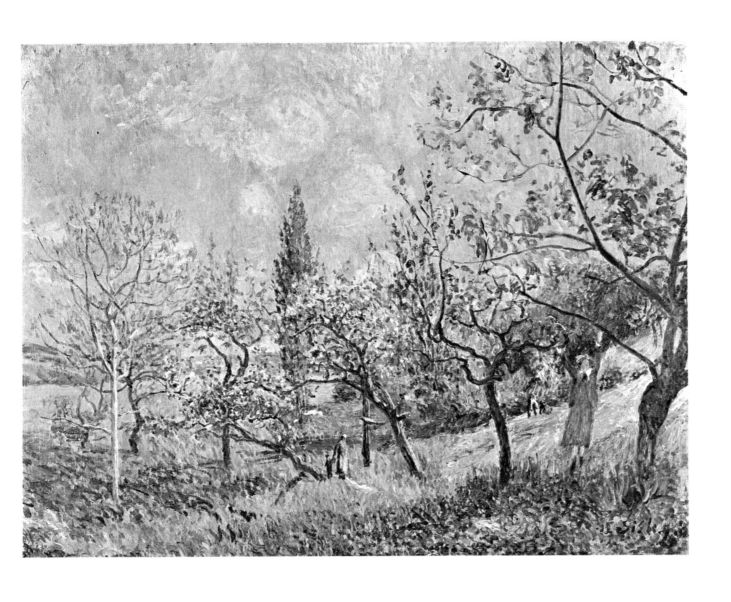

AN ORCHARD IN SPRING, 1881
Oil on canvas, $21^1/_4$" x $28^5/_{16}$" (54 x 72 cm.)
Museum Boymans van Beuningen, Rotterdam.

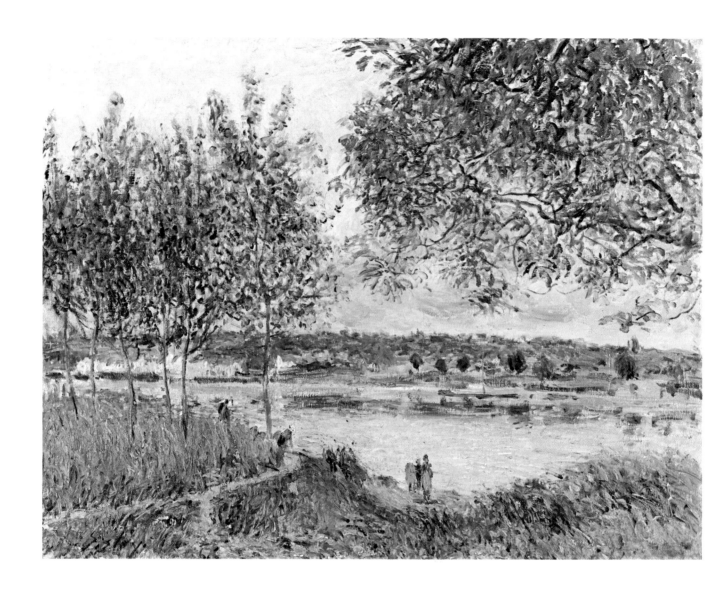

PATH TO THE OLD FERRY AT BY, around 1882
Oil on canvas, 19⁵/₈" x 25⁵/₈" (50 x 65 cm.)
Tate Gallery, London

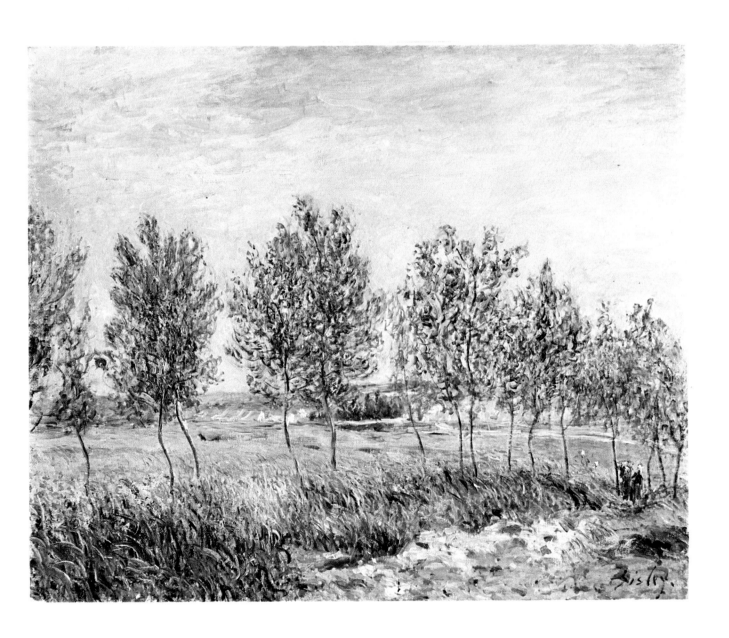

43

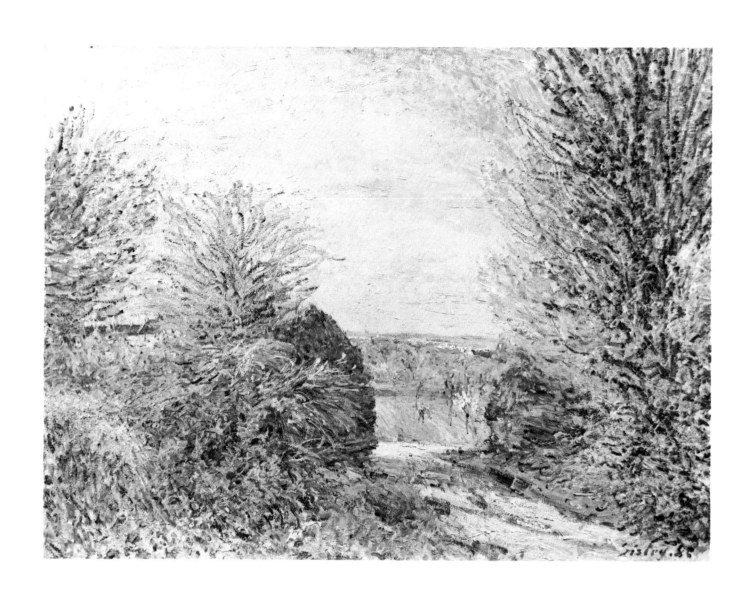

PATH OF VENEUX-NADON IN SPRING, 1885
Oil on canvas, 21^1/$_4$" x 28^3/$_4$" (54 x 73 cm.)
Private collection

SMALL MEADOWS IN SPRING · By, 1880
Oil on canvas 21³/₈" x 28³/₄" (54,3 x 73 cm.)
Tate Gallery, London

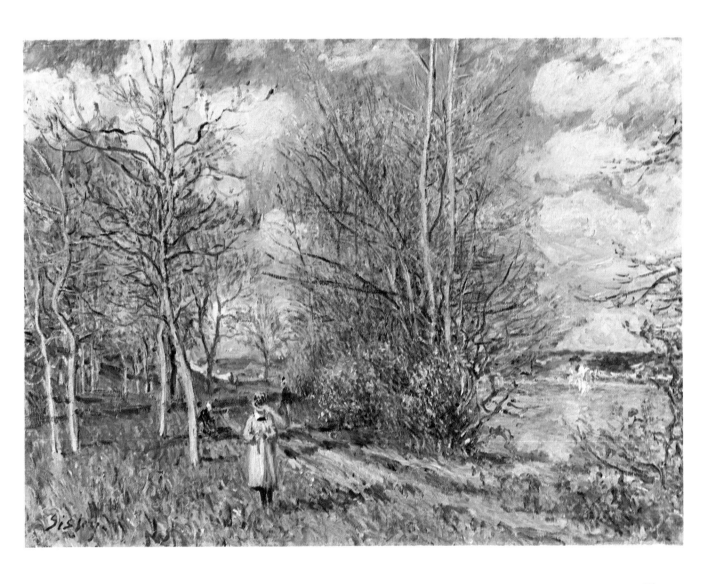

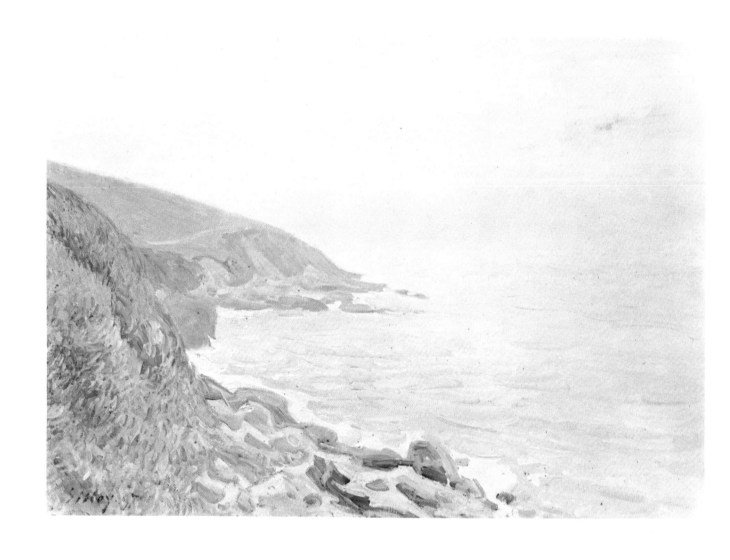

The Coast of Wales in the mist, 1897
Oil on canvas, 18$^1/_{16}$" x 23$^5/_8$" (46 x 61 cm.)
Museum of Fine Arts, Rouen

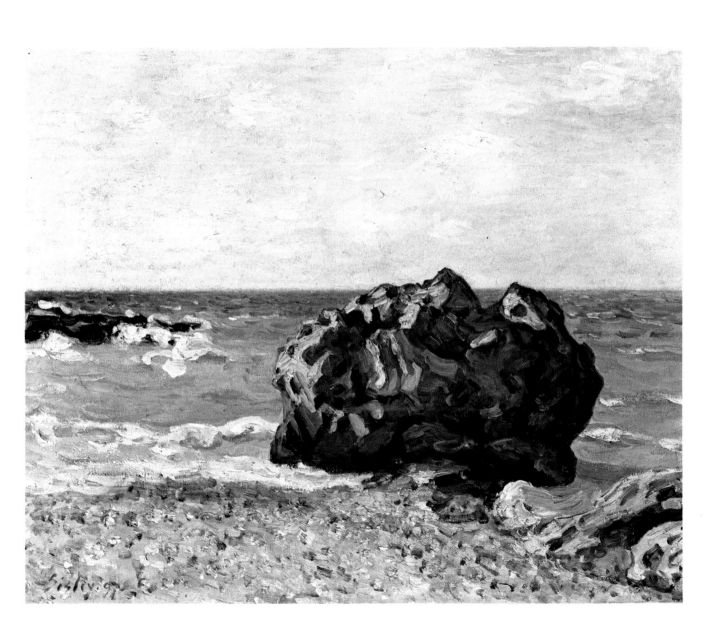

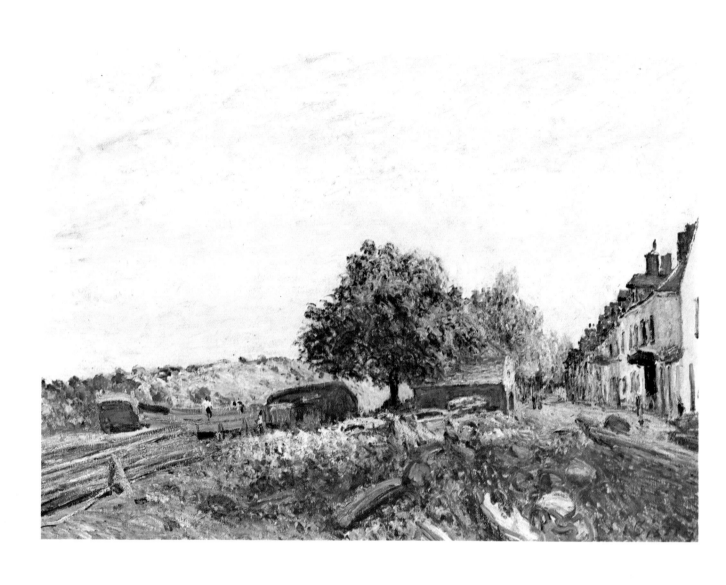

SAINT-MAMMÈS, IN THE MORNING, no date
Oil on canvas, 26³/₄" x 36" (65 x 92 cm.)
Collection: Mr. Nathan Cummings, New York

THE IMPRESSIONIST STRUGGLE (1871-80)

The years of preparation were over. Sisley's life had begun to take on a definite shape. War between France and Germany broke out on July 10, 1870. Paris was besieged and the Empire was collapsing. In 1871 France was defeated. There were rumblings of revolution, and Sisley took up residence on the outskirts of Paris, in the nearby village of Louveciennes (2 rue de la Princesse), near the home of Renoir's parents (18 route de Versailles).

There were abrupt shifts in the political climate, as well as in the daily life of the French, including changes in fashion. The artificial flower business run by Sisley's father failed and had to be abandoned, possibly because of the uncertain business outlook or unsuccessful speculation, possibly on account of his failing health, for he died shortly afterwards. Henceforth his son would be without his financial backing and would have to rely on his own work to support his family.

In his personal life, he was as much in turmoil as society as a whole. The gates of the past had closed irrevocably and those of the future had not yet revealed anything but a vague, blurred outline of what was to come. Liberal, even revolutionary forces were running out of patience, while conservative forces were divided but all the more stubborn in their determination to retain power. The prosperity and the poverty of the years after the war pitted segments of society against each other, and the resultant unrest was a common feature of daily life.

The struggle in the realm of art offered the same alternatives and highlighted the conflict between different trends and different generations. But the champions of a lightened palette had increased in number, both among artists and among the general public; the art dealer Paul Durand-Ruel, who had returned from London, where he had sought refuge during the war and had met both Monet and Pissarro, intimated that he was willing to help the young painters, perceptively seeing in them the natural successors to the painters of the Barbizon school, who until that time had been his most prized protégés.

In the autumn of 1871, at the German Gallery in London (168 New Bond Street), he showed an important collection of French paintings, featuring a landscape by Sisley, whose paintings he bought on a regular basis after 1872. Sisley's production must have increased considerably by then, for the catalogue drawn by François Daulte lists about thirty canvases for that year. This would also tend to confirm the theory that his output of the years before, when he had no dealer to handle his work, had disappeared or been lost.

This increased activity should not be attributed simply to the need to sell enough to support his family, nor to his new-found freedom, to brighter times after harsh experiences, after the anxiety and deprivation of the war years and the Paris Commune of 1870. His works produced in 1872, more than those done previously, are imbued with a quality unique to Sisley, a significant feature of his evolution, which marked a definite and definitive step forward. To realize this, one has only to study his paintings.

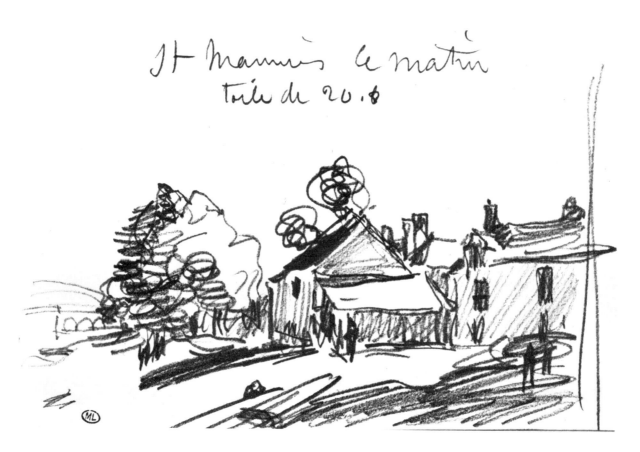

St. Mammès in the Morning, 1838-1885.
(From the Book of Drawings - Folio 35) 4³/₄" x 7¹/₂" (19 x 12 cm.) Louvre Museum, Paris

In 1870 it was already possible to discern in some of his canvases elements he would develop further in the future: the study of shimmering reflections, the treatment of great stretches of sky and water, snow in the small towns in the suburbs. In addition to these characteristics, in 1872 other prototypes appeared: two paintings depicting the floods in Port-Marly are the first attempt to handle this theme which he was to take up once more in 1876 and which he was to use as the motif of some of his most nearly perfect and successful pictures. Likewise heralding the future were three snowy landscapes which, in their treatment of light and the hazy, blurred atmosphere, marked a very clear advance over the painting of 1870. In addition, several of his works of that year, notably some large landscapes, displayed an extraordinary subtlety in Sisley's handling of light and in his depiction of the sky. By then he was clearly the master of his craft and very conscious of what he was feeling (see p. 21).

This attitude of the artist towards nature was to be characteristic of the new school of painters and was to give rise to opposition from advocates of other trends. Perhaps, without being fully conscious of it and certainly without announcing it to the world, Sisley was already expressing his opposition to the credos of his elders, including those who preceded him in stressing the importance of landscape art. Like his friends, he took this position because he had a fundamental belief that the artist should capture the outward aspects of familiar scenes and the fleeting changes in everyday life, his aim being to perpetuate the ephemeral and evanescent moment.

This vision was quite contrary to everything that had been done up until that time, even by the Barbizon painters, especially Théodore Rousseau, who was devoted to the pursuit of what was permanent rather than passing. By the patient observation of details, Rousseau eliminated chance and the transitory and regarded only the lasting aspects of nature. He painted the life of the earth, whereas Sisley painted light, and a land caught on the fly as its very outlines were momentarily changed. He did not depict the material composition of things but their radiance (see p. 33).

The contrast between what survived of the past and what heralded the future was destined to become more and more accentuated and would henceforth be expressed not

St. Mammès, 1838-1885.
(From the Book of Drawings - Folio 52) 4³/₄" x 7¹/₂" (19 x 12 cm.) Louvre Museum, Paris

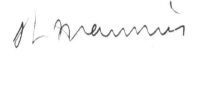

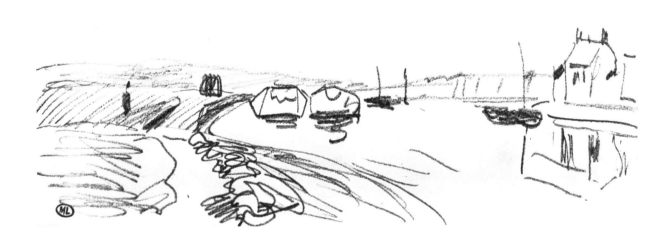

only in art but also in actuality. We must stress that hostile acts were provoked not by the artists of the new school but by the people, artists and public alike, who resisted change.

For years the young artists who were accused of scorning tradition had in fact respected it and had continued to submit their works for consideration by the selection committee of the official Salon, who almost always rejected them. In the hope of earning a livelihood and discovering new sponsors, the painters had kept aloof from public demonstrations but, faced with the silent opposition of the government to their request to revive the idea of the Salon of 1863, they reluctantly concluded that they would have to consider organizing an exhibition themselves.

When they had their first such exhibition in 1874, when they affirmed their unity as a group, fully conscious of what they were seeking and in complete command of their artistic skills, they aroused a storm of jeers and insults which their critics sought to sum up by describing them as « Impressionists. »

Even though Sisley had had two paintings accepted by the Salon of 1870, since that

The Banks of the Loing, 1890.
Etching, 5¹/₂" x 8⁵/₈" (14 x 22 cm.) Bibliothèque Nationale, Paris

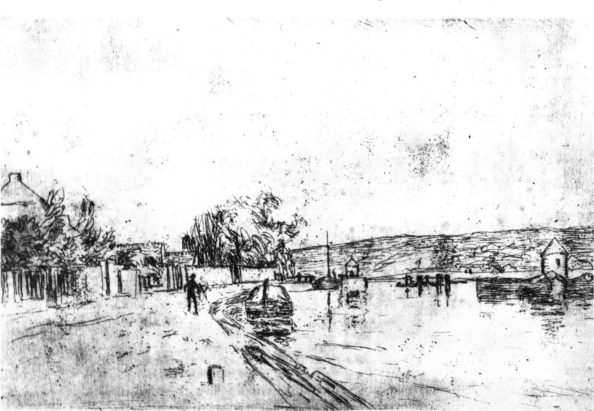

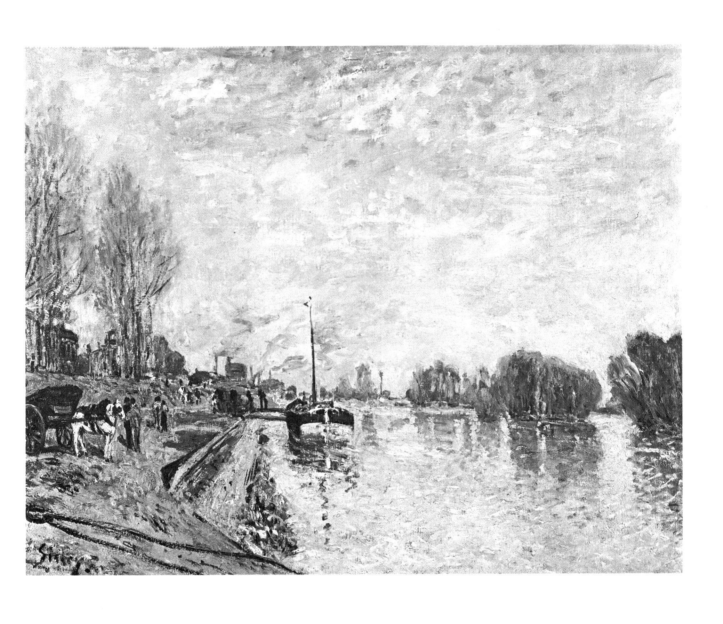

THE SEINE AT SURESNES, 1879
Oil on canvas, 20" x 25$^1/_2$" (50 x 65 cm.)
Private collection, New York

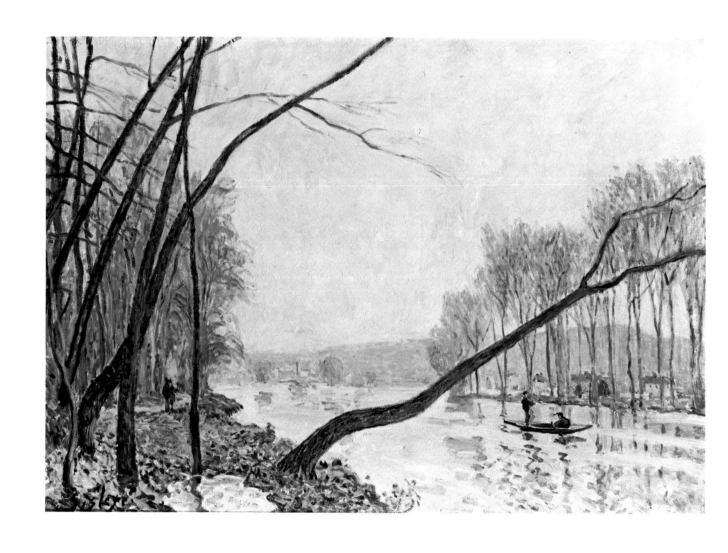

Banks of the Seine in the fall, 1876
Oil on canvas, $18^{1}/_{16}$" x $25^{5}/_{8}$" (46 x 65 cm.)
Staedelsches Kunstinstitut, Frankfurt

Sand heaps, 1875
Oil on canvas, 21$^1/_4$" x 25$^7/_8$" (54 x 65,7 cm.)
The Art Institute of Chicago
Mr. and Mrs. Martin A. Ryerson Collection

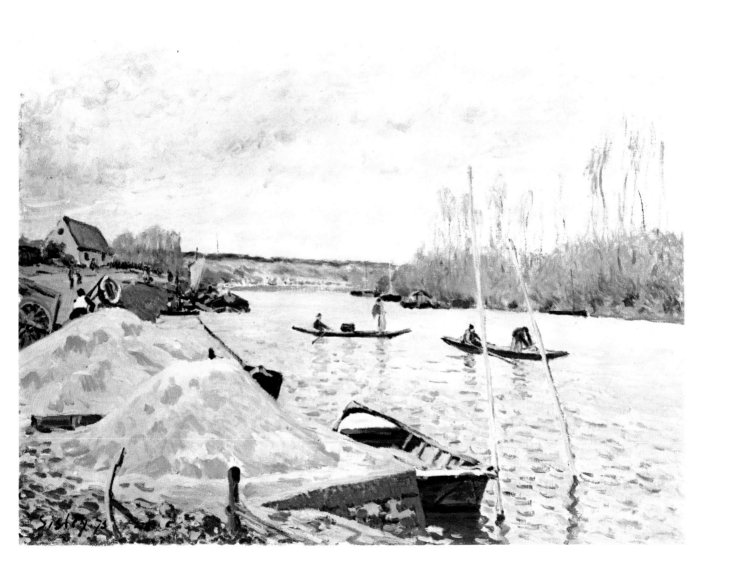

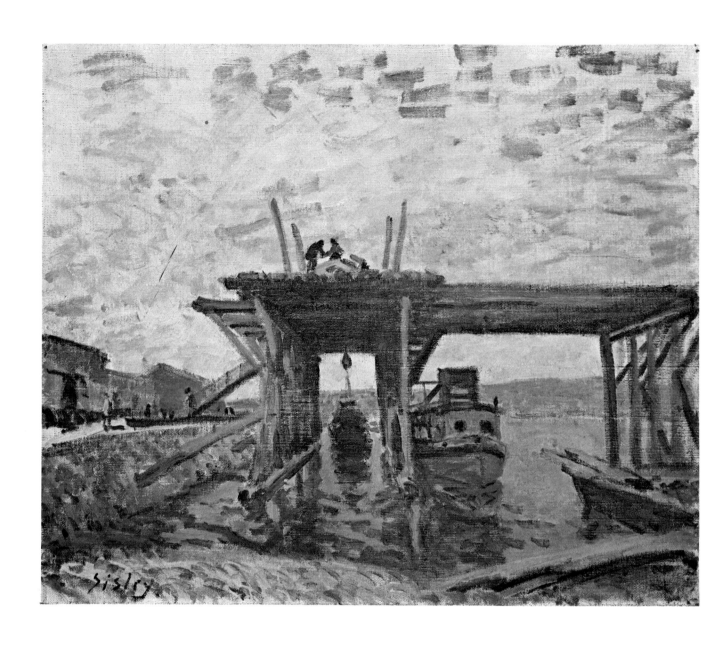

BRIDGE UNDER CONSTRUCTION, 1885
Oil on canvas, $18^1/_{16}$ x $21^5/_8$" (46 x 55 cm.)
Museum Ordrupgaard, Copenhagen

time the paintings he submitted had been refused. He decided that in the future he would wholeheartedly participate in the activities of the Impressionist group, and in fact did so on a regular basis, that is to say in 1874, 1876 and 1877. He did not appear in 1879, 1880 and 1881 and showed again for the last time in 1882; he did not participate in the eighth and last exhibition in 1886.

In the course of these years the composition of the original group gradually changed, sometimes rather drastically, as when the last showings included new trends and new techniques, notably those of Gauguin and of Seurat.

Sisley would not allow himself to be tempted and did not depart from the line he had drawn for himself some years back. He was to make a last effort to renew contact with officialdom and the general public; in 1879, he once more presented his works to the selection committee of the Salon and was rejected.

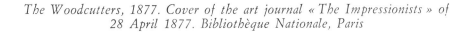

*The Woodcutters, 1877. Cover of the art journal « The Impressionists » of
28 April 1877. Bibliothèque Nationale, Paris*

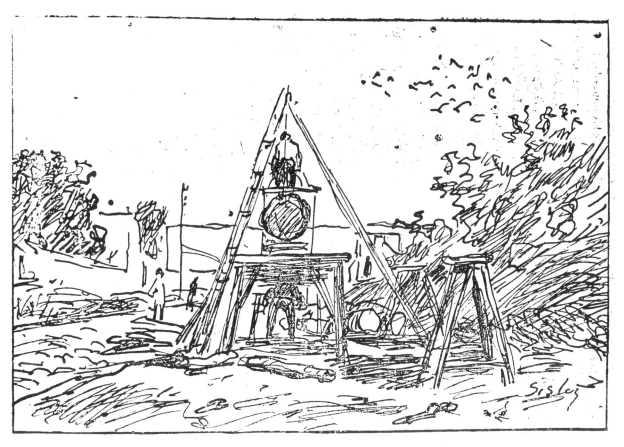

Scieurs de long, croquis de M. SISLEY, d'après son tableau.

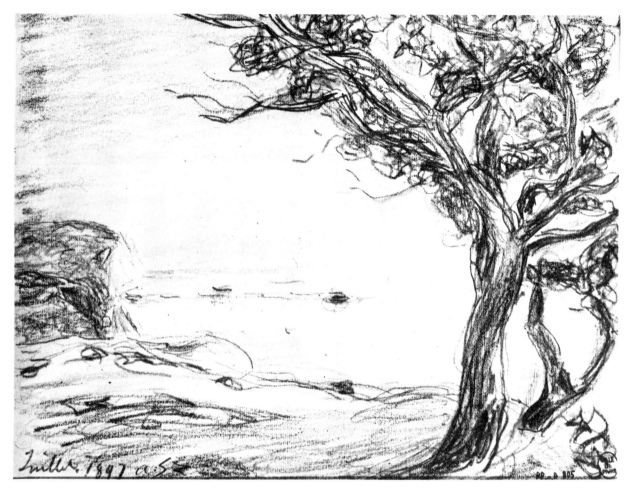

Trees at the Seaside. The Bay of Cardiff, 1897.
Colored pencil on paper, 6¹/₄" x 8¹/₄" (16 x 21 cm.) Museum of the Petit-Palais, Paris

The hard times continued. Yet his ideas and his work continued on their chosen path and progressed. Connoisseurs who admired his art grew less rare, the sarcasm directed against him less biting. The Salon itself was influenced by the very works it had rejected. If it continued to reject the innovators, it opened its doors to their followers, and one began to see displayed more and more paintings using luminous colors and a freer technique. Some dealers indicated that they were tempted to take the path Durand-Ruel had blazed.

Within the next ten years the Impressionists, as much as a result of the attacks against them as of the praises for them, would develop an identity sufficiently striking as to oblige the public to take stock of their contribution to the artistic life of the day. One factor in this belated recognition was the disappearance from the scene, within a short time, of some of their chief predecessors in stressing landscape painting. Théodore Rousseau died in 1867; Corot and Millet in 1875, Diaz in 1876; Daubigny in 1878. Their deaths and the echoes they awakened proved that their ideas had captivated a rather large public and that landscapes appealed to an ever-growing number of art lovers.

Yet in spite of some success and temporary encouragement given notably to Renoir and Monet, the financial situation of the group as a whole remained exceedingly precarious. Soon Durand-Ruel, whose acquaintance Sisley had made in 1872 through Monet and Pissarro, could no longer sustain the financial assistance he had been giving, and Sisley, deprived of this help since 1877, would not be able to count on it until 1880.

His plight became so desperate that Sisley, finding himself unable to make both ends meet, frequently had to ask for assistance, not from his painter friends who were as short of funds as he, but from some connoisseurs who had confidence in him and refused to be stampeded by the current lack of appreciation of the artist. Among them were the critic Théodore Duret, who was one of the first to write about the Impressionists and who in 1878 published a book on them (in which he did not fail to mention Sisley); the publisher Georges Charpentier, whose friendship was particularly strong and helpful, especially in the case of Renoir; the baker and restaurant owner Murer, whose restaurant at 95 boulevard Voltaire was open almost every Wednesday to Sisley, Renoir, Monet, Pissarro and Guillaumin. By 1887 he owned twenty-eight of Sisley's paintings, a convincing testimony of the steadfastness of his admiration.

Another friendly gesture came to him in 1874, when, thanks to an invitation from baritone Jean-Baptiste Faure, a great art lover and one of the first champions of Impressionism, Sisley was able to spend four months in England, from July to October, and brought back with him (again according to the Daulte catalogue) about fifteen paintings. In spite of their artistic merit, they would not add appreciably to our knowledge of this artist's work but for the fact that two of them, depicting the bridge at Hampton Court, are of an interesting composition, the proportions of the foreground serving to accentuate a perspective behind it fading into the distance (see pp. 26, 27).

Apart from his friendships and the routine of daily life, Sisley pursued a course in his work that did not seem to be influenced by events. The work was sufficient unto itself, displaying an improving technique, as he continued to select the same themes and treated them in the same manner. As has been said, the work was dominated by landscapes with wide and distant horizons, with a great deal of sky and water visible (see p. 53). Yet it was during the years 1873-76 that Sisley painted, especially in Louveciennes, a few landscapes turned in on themselves: narrow streets, or rather lanes slipping between houses and gardens; scenes as intimate and homely as the interiors of bourgeois apartments (see p. 25).

The snowy landscapes are of the same sort, imbued with silence; the first were done as early as 1872, in Louveciennes, the later ones in 1875-76 in Marly (see p. 24). Perhaps it is also possible to see in these paintings the desire to retain something unusual and fleeting, just as did the flood scenes, done first in 1872 and depicted again in 1876 (see p. 38, 39). In this same category, we should point out, are Claude Monet's views of the Gare Saint-Lazare, also dated 1876.

Faced with ever-increasing difficulties, Sisley's character underwent a decided change. The affable youth had turned into a morose man, and his cheerful disposition was clouded by anxiety. Without being aggressive, he no longer possessed the sweetness and friendliness which all those who had known him in his youth had valued. Shy and worried, he was less capable of withstanding hardship than Monet, Renoir or Pissarro, and circumstances were such that he was offered few moments of hope. Yet he never considered giving up.

In 1880 he had reason to believe that things might change for the better. Several events occured which promised to change his situation and to end the monotonous string of misfortunes which for almost ten years, had held out to him the prospect of a future of nothing but relentless poverty.

Support for Sisley and his friends became more widespread and their future prospects could be expected to be less grim. Durand-Ruel began to buy again. Publisher

The Banks of the Loing, the Cart, 1890.
Etching, 5³/₈" x 8³/₈" (13,5 x 21,5 cm.) Bibliothèque Nationale, Paris

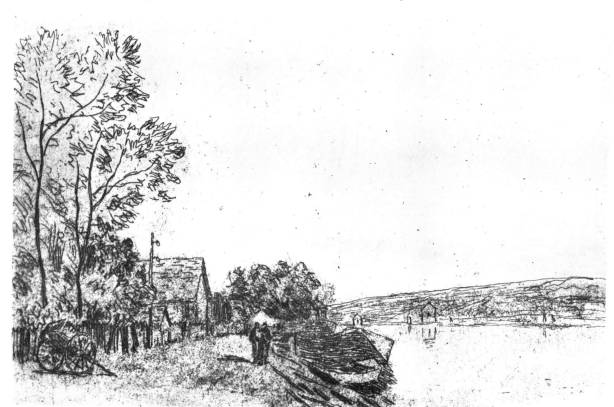

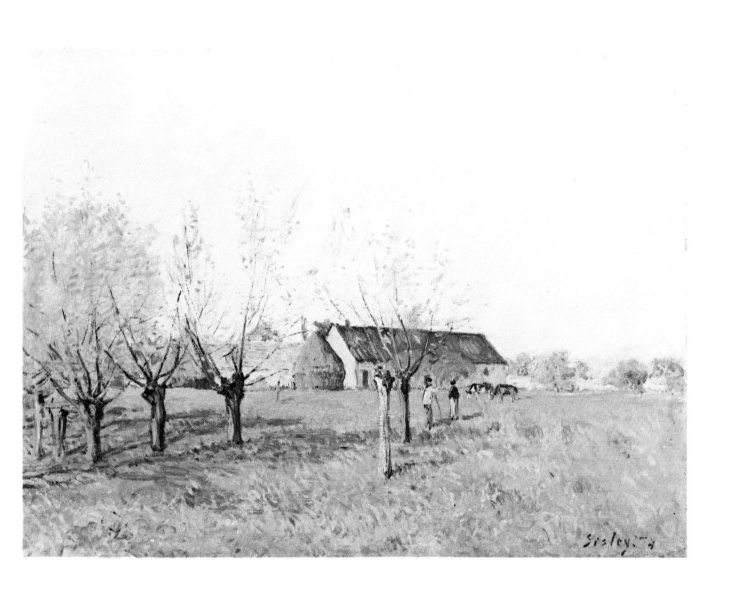

FARMHOUSE. LE TROU D'ENFER, 1874
Oil on canvas, 18¹/₂" x 24" (47 x 62 cm.)
Private Collection

THE SEINE AT BOUGIVAL, 1876
Oil on canvas, 17⁷/₈" x 23⁵/₈" (45 x 61 cm.)
Private Collection

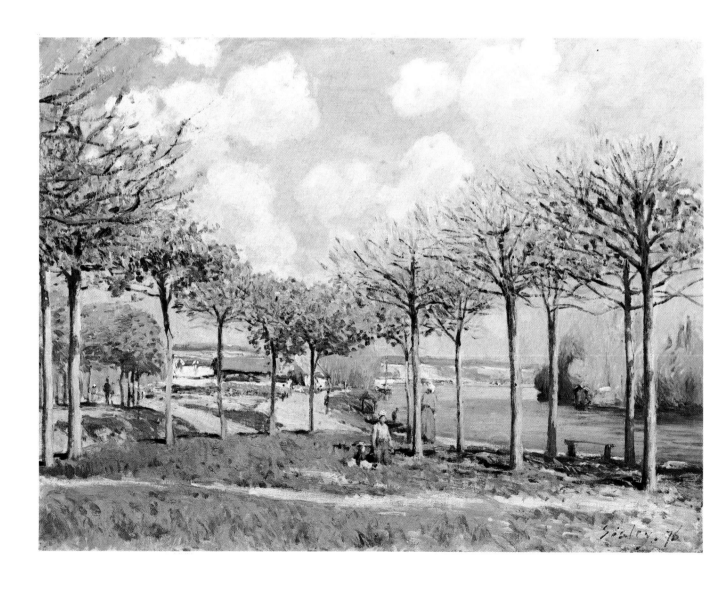

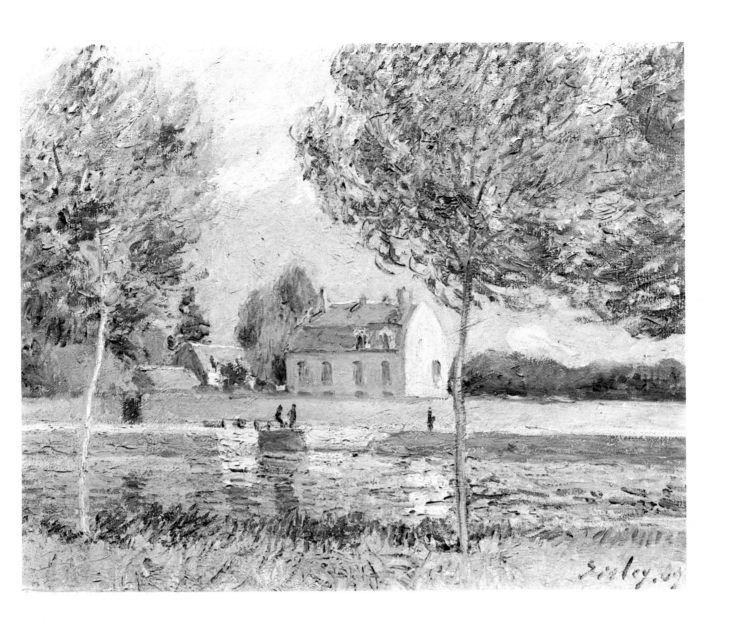

HOUSES ALONG THE LOING, 1889
Oil on canvas, $12^7/_8$" x $14^7/_8$" (33 x 41 cm.)
Private Collection

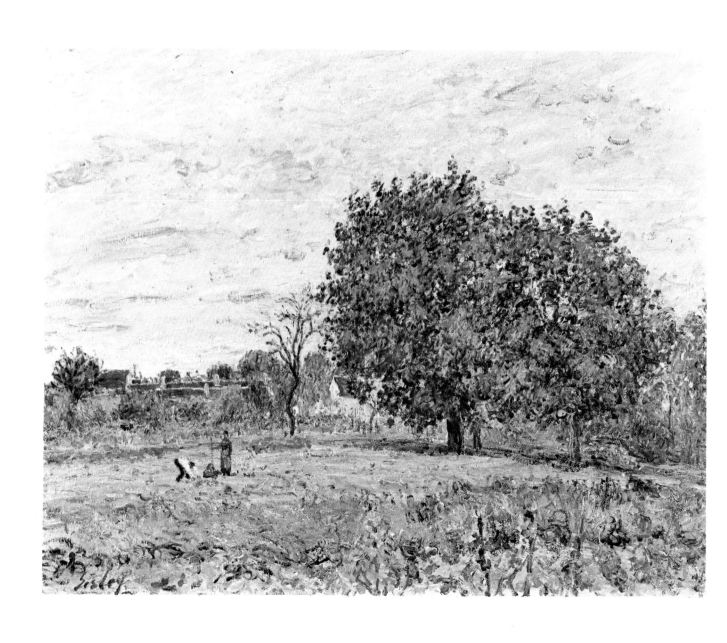

NUT TREES SUNSET, around 1882
Oil on canvas, 36¹/₄" x 28³/₄" (73 x 92 cm.)
Collection: David Findlay Galleries, New York

Georges Charpentier, who for some years had been able to obtain for Renoir some portrait commissions from wealthy families (the Cahens of Antwerp, the Bérards and a few others), decided to organize major showings of the works of the artists whom he admired, in a new gallery, « La Vie Moderne » (Modern Life). In 1879 he exhibited an important collection of Renoir's paintings. In 1880 he offered the walls of the gallery to Monet. In 1881, it was the turn of Sisley, who exhibited fourteen paintings.

In 1878 Renoir had successfully begun to submit his paintings to the Salon. Then, in 1880, a painting by Monet was shown. Encouraged by this, Sisley also submitted pictures to the Salon, in 1879, but was rejected. Renoir continued to be well received during the following years (1881, 1882, 1883). He traveled: he went to Italy, to Algeria, and at the same time started gradually to withdraw from Impressionism as he acquired increasing recognition. Sisley also moved from place to place but did not change his style. Since the end of the war he had successively lived in Louveciennes, Marly (beginning in 1875) (see cover) and Sèvres (beginning in 1877). In 1880, or perhaps as early as 1879, he settled in Veneux-Nadon, near Moret-sur-Loing (see p. 44).

In June 1881 he once again paid a brief visit to England, to the Isle of Wight, where he planned to work, for he wrote to Paul Durand-Ruel in a letter dated June 9: « I went for a few walks on the island and I shall start working as soon as I get some canvas ». Before he had time to collect his painting materials, he had to go back to France, to which he therefore returned without any new works.

From then on he was not to leave Moret and its vicinity except on two occasions. During the summer of 1894, he paid a visit to Rouen, staying first at the Hôtel du Dauphin (4 place de la République) which then was being run by Eugène Murer, the former restaurateur of the boulevard Voltaire, and later at the house of François Despeaux, an industrialist and collector. This gave him the opportunity to paint the Normandy countryside but his themes remained his usual ones (see p. 66). They changed, however, during a later visit of four months he paid to England in 1897 through the generosity of François Despeaux. He brought back from his trip several seascapes, the only ones he ever painted (see pp. 46, 47).

Even though he moved quite frequently in his earlier life, he remained in the same area, the center of which was Saint-Mammès, to the north of Moret, where the Loing flows into the Seine (see pp. 48, 63). Within a radius of three or four miles, in Veneux-les-Sablons, then in Champagne and Thomery, Sisley was untiring in the study of the changing seasons and of light, often coming back to the same places, never weary of looking at nature and without displaying any desire to cease this contemplation. Perhaps one reason for this repetition of experience, it might even be called his « constancy », was the fact that, unlike his friends, he had not had the good fortune to make a reputation for himself. He continued to live on the thin edge of destitution, frequently obliged to borrow modest sums of money to help him through his difficult stretches, to pay his rent or his moving expenses.

However, he continued to paint and exhibited regularly. The big retrospective show

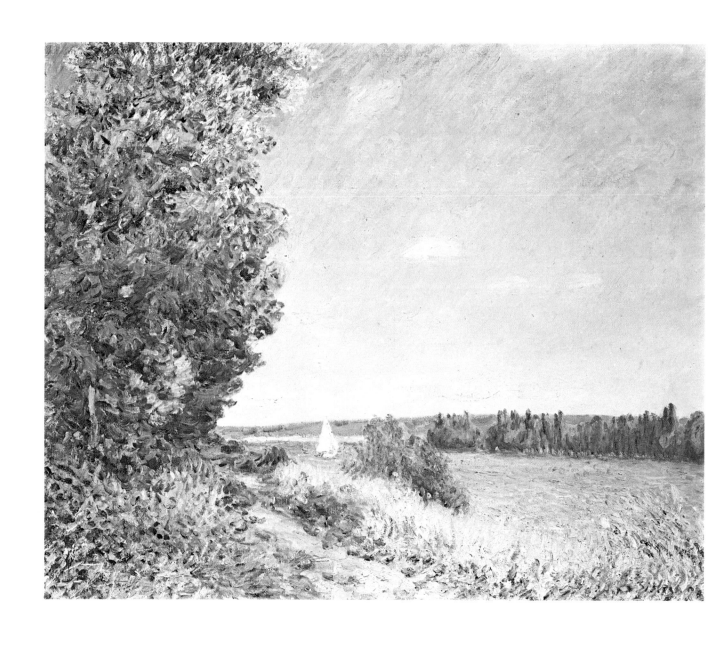

NORMANDY, THE PATH ALONG THE WATER AT SAHURS, IN
THE EVENING, 1894
Oil on canvas, $31^7/_8$ x $39^3/_8$" (81 x 100 cm.)
Museum of Fine Arts, Rouen

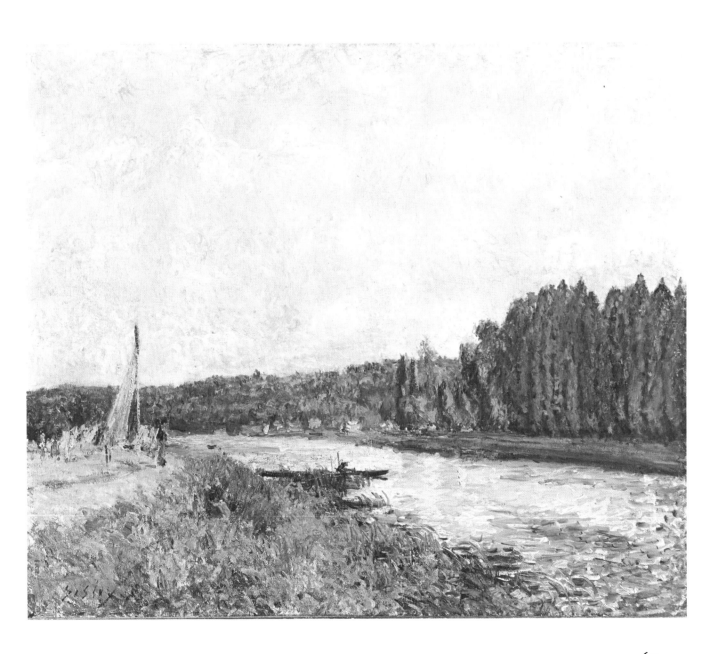

which Durand-Ruel arranged for him in 1883 (seventy pictures) was not very successful and did nothing to change his unhappy lot. His admission, as an associate member, to the young « Société nationale des Beaux-Arts » in 1890, was sponsored by Alfred Roll, and he was to exhibit there almost every year afterwards, but this too failed to benefit him financially.

Yet he was not discouraged, and up to 1885 his production remained fairly steady. From 1886 on it began to decline, although it was still respectable up to 1892. Suddenly, in 1893, his output became much scarcer. From then on he never regained his former energy. Yet one last hope seemed to be justified: in 1897, Georges Petit showed a hundred and forty-six of his paintings and six pastel drawings in a new, enormous retrospective exhibition. The press took very little notice of it, and collectors were not tempted to buy.

His wife fell ill and died in October 1898. He himself felt that he was failing, and no change of scene was able to relieve his depression. He developed cancer of the throat, which became steadily worse, and he resigned himself to his illness with a great deal of courage.

The Banks of the Loing. Houses on the Waterfront, 1890
Etching, 5⁵/₈" x 9" (14,5 x 22,5 cm.) Bibliothèque Nationale, Paris

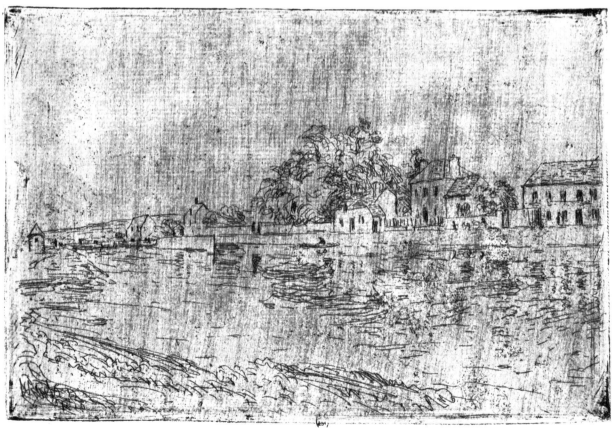

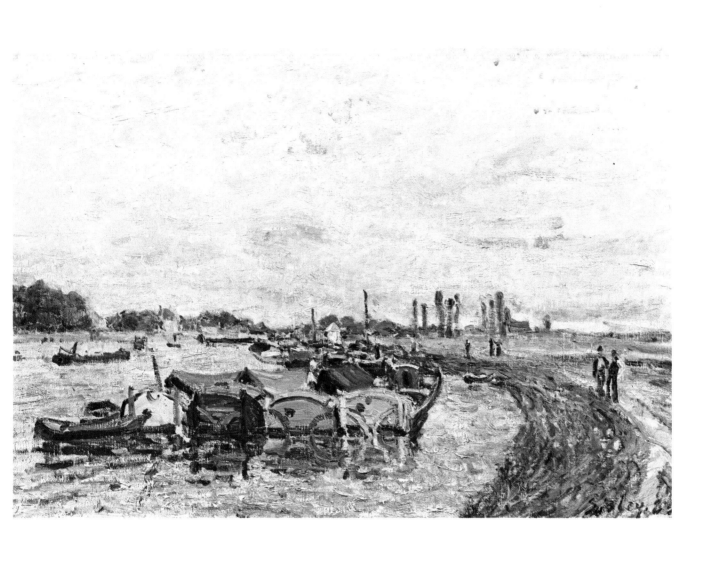

Barges at Saint-Mammès, 1885
Oil on canvas, 15" x 21⁵/₈" (38 x 55 cm.)
Private Collection

69

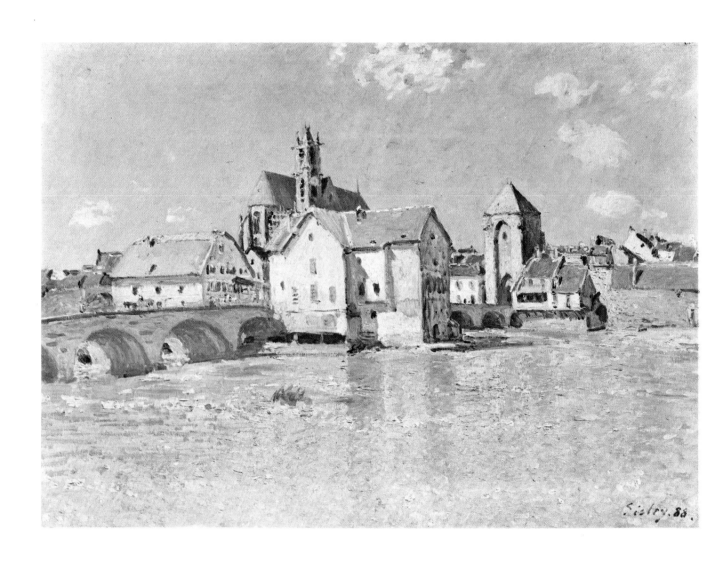

THE BRIDGE AT MORET. MORNING SUN, 1888
Oil canvas, 25^5/$_8$" x 36" (65 x 92 cm.)
Private Collection

70

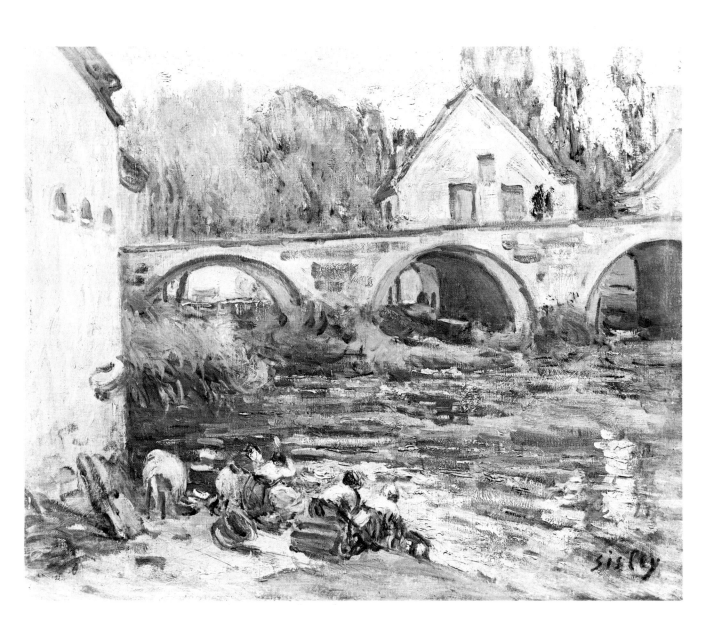

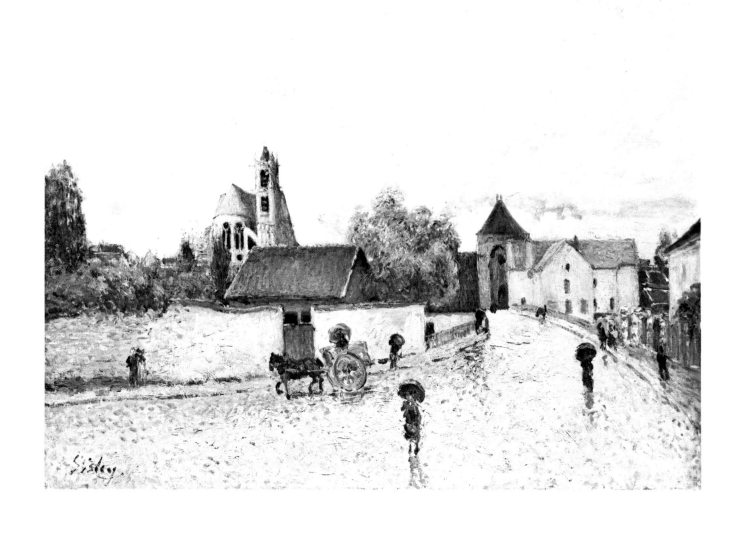

MORET-SUR-LOING. RAINY WEATHER, 1887-88
Oil on canvas, 21³/₈" x 28³/₄" (54 x 73 cm.)
Private Collection

The letters he wrote to Doctor Viau on the subject are truly heartbreaking. « I can no longer fight, my dear friend; I am at the end of my tether. » And the next day: « Pay no attention to anything I said in my letter yesterday. The weakness has passed. » And on January 13, 1899: « My pain puts me on the rack. I have no energy left to fight it. » He died on January 29 and was buried in the Moret cemetery on February 1.

The history of Sisley and his art does not stop there. In February the Bernheim-Jeune Gallery exhibited fourteen of his most recent pictures. In March, Durand-Ruel had a similar showing of twenty-eight paintings in New York. A little later, on May 1, an auction was held at the Hôtel Drouot to raise money for Sisley's two children. Twenty-seven of his paintings fetched the unexpected sum of 112,320 francs. Finally, on March 6, 1900, in a sale of the Adolphe Tavernier collection at the Hôtel Drouot, the price of the canvas of 1876 depicting the flood at Marly was raised by Count Isaac de Camondo to 43,000 francs, a staggering amount for a painting at the time (see p. 38).

The success which nothing had permitted the artist to hope for during his lifetime had finally been achieved. The fact that it was just too late for him to enjoy it adds a last sad note to the story of a man who, by virtue of his decency, his sensitivity and his talent, might have seemed predestined to live out a full and happy life, enjoying the fruits of his labor. Yet in spite of his misfortunes, he managed to put into his work all of the light, the serenity and the exquisite benevolence which were so much a part of him and, by his unremitting courage, to achieve that work in the face of disappointment and adversity.

III. SISLEY'S ART

Sisley's art, like his life, was a blend of moderation and modesty, without violent contrasts or any taking of strong stands. Even when fate suddenly deprived him of an income that could have assured him a life free from financial worries, his paintings give no sign of this. If one tries to find in them something special and distinctive, one is struck by the logic of an evolution which does not seek to surprise and which calmly progresses at its own pace.

Renoir, after a few years during which he remained loyal to the creed of Impressionism, voluntarily cast it aside to take another road. As soon as he found it possible to do so, Cézanne left the ranks to create his own personal vision and technique. Degas was linked to Impressionism only by fortuitous circumstances, and therefore his allegiance was tenuous. But just as the ties of these artists to Impressionism were loose and temporary, so, too, did Sisley, along with Monet and Pissarro, represent the opposite attitude: they were a part of Impressionism when it was born and as it developed throughout the seventies. However, a few years later, even Pissarro tried to experiment further in practicing the Pointillism employed by Seurat. Claude Monet also went beyond Impres-

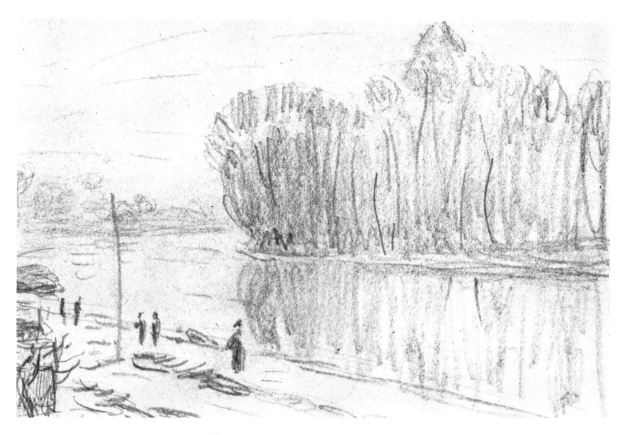

The Loing Canal. Morning, no date.
Black pencil on yellow paper, 7³/₈" x 9⁷/₈" (18,7 x 25 cm.) Museum of the Petit-Palais, Paris

sionism in his series of *Waterlilies* where the frenzy of color transcended physical reality to enter the domain of abstraction. Only Sisley belonged totally and completely, through his temperament and his conception of art, to Impressionism in its truest and most absolute form. He was loyal to it and he was its most authentic representative.

For him, Impressionism was not an attitude to be adopted, a sterile formula dictated by the ideas and the movements of the period. It was an accurate and sincere expression of his nature; the proof of this is that the artist never sought to break away and try to find other routes to success. Never did he exhibit any desire to startle or surprise, or manifest the anxiety of those who try endlessly to renew themselves. If he had not been rejected by the selection committees, he would have been glad to continue to exhibit in the official Salons. He was so consistent and unobtrusive that often he can best be explained by comparison with other painters.

Thus in order to demark stages in his work and the varied points of view in his art, or simply to define the work, Sisley's themes must be dissected and his treatment of subjects must be compared with that of his fellow Impressionists. In spite of that, even if the differences between the themes are emphasized, it is impossible to deny the remarkable unity of his work. The motifs are few in number and are almost exclusively

74

landscapes. According to François Daulte's catalogue, apart from landscapes, Sisley painted only nine still lifes, one dual portrait and two indoor scenes.

As for the still lifes, four of them were produced in the very early years, probably in 1867 (Sisley's first known painting is dated 1865). They are not very significant as heralds of what Impressionist painting was to become, but they show a sense of order and composition. However, *Still Life with Pheasant* is interesting because Sisley painted the plumage with soft, separate brush strokes — a technique that ultimately became one of the characteristic features of Impressionism.

In a bouquet of flowers done about 1875, the artist's touch is freer and the result more shimmering. Two other still lifes (of fruits) are admirable in their composition (see p. 77 and cover) and demonstrate a greater mastery of the medium and therefore were probably produced at a later date. Finally there are two pictures of 1888, each representing a pike. These works, however unusual their subjects, do not mark a great esthetic advance on Sisley's part, but the last four (the fruit and the fish) use a perspective in depth such as Sisley had not employed for his landscapes, which were always observed at normal eye level.

The Banks of the Loing near St. Mammès, no date.
Lithograph, 5¹/₂" x 8⁵/₈" (13,5 x 22 cm.) Bibliothèque Nationale, Paris

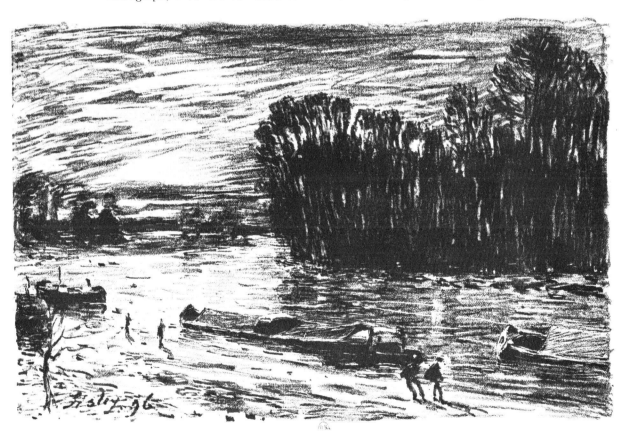

The double portrait is dated 1871 and depicts the artist's two children. In it we are already conscious of the important role played by light, which enlivens the surface of everything, even inert objects, such as furniture or clothes. But there is not the same effect of lively light so noticeable in the brilliant landscapes; neither is there the same feeling of space which Sisley gave through his use of color, rather than by the use of fleeing perspectives.

The two indoor scenes are the *Smithy at Marly* and the *Farm Room,* dated respectively 1875 and 1880. Both appear to be fairly unusual and atypical experiments. They permitted the artist to observe and translate into artistic terms the clear contrasts of shadow and light, to demonstrate the effects of chiaroscuro and of a foreshortened perspective on the ground and on the ceiling. But Sisley was too accustomed to the open air to feel completely at ease in a confined setting, and his interiors express an oppressive heaviness.

Evidently, it was in landscape painting that Sisley expressed himself the most completely and in which he quickly attained mastery of his craft. Landscapes seemed to him so rich and suggestive that he often returned to the same location to observe and note the differences brought about by changes in hours and in the seasons. He does not seek to modify the angle of vision, nor does he seek to imitate himself. He is somewhat like Monet painting the Rouen cathedral or haystacks. But Sisley is not striving to give an impression of instability and even of the dissolution of matter in the changing light. He neither scorns nor underestimates the finite structure of a landscape that interest him.

Even in his early works, he shows a concern for the structure of space. His subjects were not chosen because of their picturesque or anecdotal character. However natural it may be, a Sisley landscape invariably has a well thought out composition, is carefully constructed and has a strict orderliness which is almost architectural. There is nothing haphazard about it. Possibly it is a direct result of what the artist learned from Corot's paintings.

Often the foreground is especially important, forming a very definite contrast with what is happening in the distance. A long oblique line may start in the foreground (denoting the direction taken by a road or a piece of land) and cross the width of the whole picture, from one end to the other, to lead rapidly to the horizon line. Sometimes, however, the principal subject of the painting is in the exact center, in which case there are two oblique lines that start at the bottom of the canvas and join at the center. They are created by rows of houses or trees that emplasize the rapid course of the perspective, as in the marvelous canvas of the Louvre, *The Road to Sèvres, Louveciennes* (1873), which is so typical of Sisley's art and illustrates magnificently his sense of space and light (see pp. 80, 81).

Space as conceived by Sisley takes account of the three dimension. The third is embodied in the flight toward the horizon, suggesting extensions of its movement to the right and to the left, and creates the effect of an open window which has sometimes been used to define Impressionism. In spite of this openness, the treatment of forms adopted by the artist to suggest nature corresponds quite closely to the principles of traditional Italian perspectives, confirmed by protography. However, Sisley adds something less

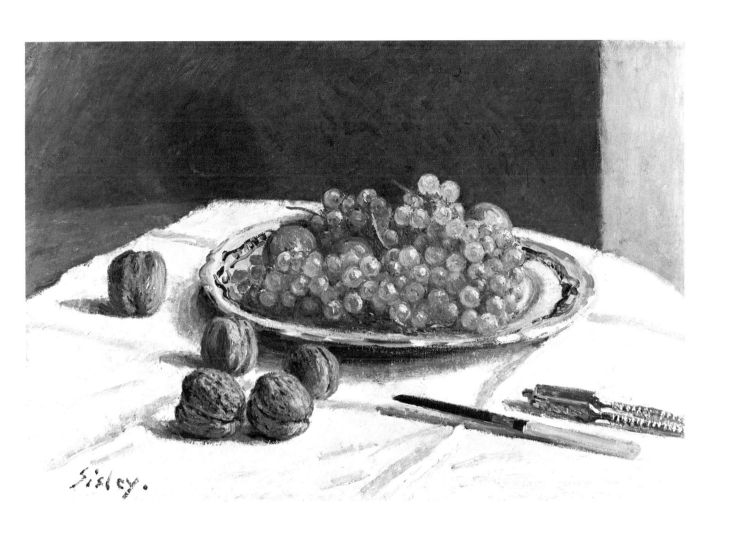

GRAPES AND WALNUTS, no date
Oil on canvas, 15" x 21³/₄" (38 x 55.5 cm.)
Museum of Fine Arts, Boston,
Bequest of John T. Spaulding

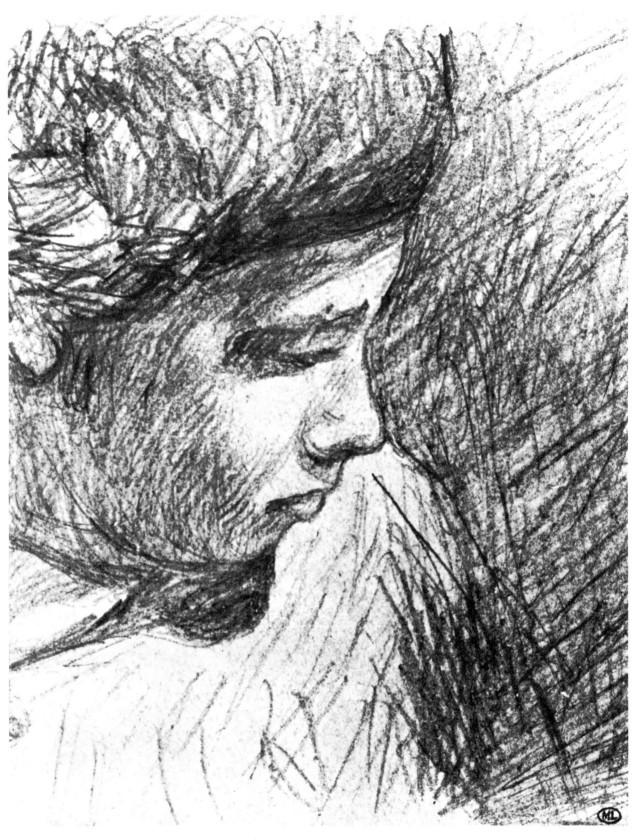

Head of a Young Boy, no date.
Black pencil, 8" x 6¹/₄" (20,5 x 15,8 cm.) Louvre Museum, Paris

rigorously scientific, a way of entering into the landscape which means that the spectator does not remain inside the subject being portrayed.

In the classical and romantic pictures of the period we see a spectacle unfolding before our eyes, we are looking at what is happening on a stage. With the Impressionists, and especially in the case of Sisley, the spectator himself is an actor in the spectacle and feels himself enveloped in its atmosphere. He is not subject to the limitations imposed by a frame but has the sensation that the boundaries of the scene may expand at any time. This is the exact opposite of an academically structured painting.

In a few instances Sisley forgoes this aerial and distant concept of space and demonstrates that he has been tempted to accept a more intimate vision. The most typical example of this sort of experiment is the series of paintings, a dozen canvases, which he produced in 1893-94, depicting the church in Moret, paintings which were at once alike and different according to the hour, the season, the weather.

In all these variations the edifice is seen from the same angle and at the same distance. Its mass practically fills the whole surface of the canvas. The church at first glance appears to have no perspective, but has in fact a perspective so weighty as to be crushing. The perspective goes into the far distance, suggested rather than seen on the extreme left side of the composition and thus preventing the whole from giving the impression of a world entirely closed unto itself (see pp. 82, 83).

This series on the church in Moret illustrates perhaps best the way the artist utilizes the contrast between shadow and light, although he does it with restraint and moderation. He does not bear down too much to produce this sort of effect. Light in Sisley's paintings is not formally divided into zones of clarity and contrasting dark shadows to establish the rhythm of space; it is everywhere the same and retains its aerial purity, its physical reality, without being the object of theatrical effects or sentimentality.

This impression of purity and of radiant light in the landscape is undoubtedly the result of the importance given to the sky, which fills at least half of the canvas in most instances. Without going so far as to imitate Jongkind or Boudin, whose skies fill two-thirds of their pictures, sometimes more, leaving only a long, narrow, horizontal strip to mark the earth, Sisley never paints a landscape closed in on itself or straightened into vertical lines as Claude Monet occasionally does in his waterlily basins. With Sisley, the placing on the canvas of the elements in the landscape is always natural. Unlike Jongkind or Boudin, for whom the sky, its changing aspects, its movement, its luminosity, are the central motif, Sisley looks at a place, expresses its atmosphere, captures its nuances, but is not solely interested in that atmosphere.

In Claude Monet's paintings the light assails concrete objects and impregnates them until it threatens to dissolve them. The stones of the cathedral of Rouen are as immaterial and unsubstantial as the flowers or the water of the Giverny pond. In Sisley's case, the houses are still visibly made of stone, the trees consist of bark and leaves, even when the painter strives to detail the effects of the passing hours on the same subject. If it is a house bathed by waters in *Floods at Port-Marly,* if it is the bridge of Moret or the

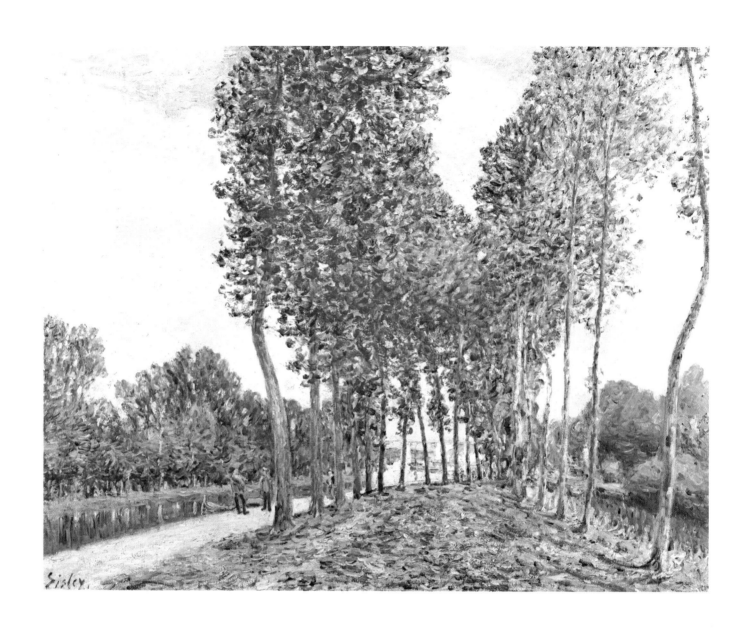

THE RIVER LOING NEAR MORET, 1892
Oil on canvas, 28³/₄" x 36" (73 x 92 cm.)
Private Collection

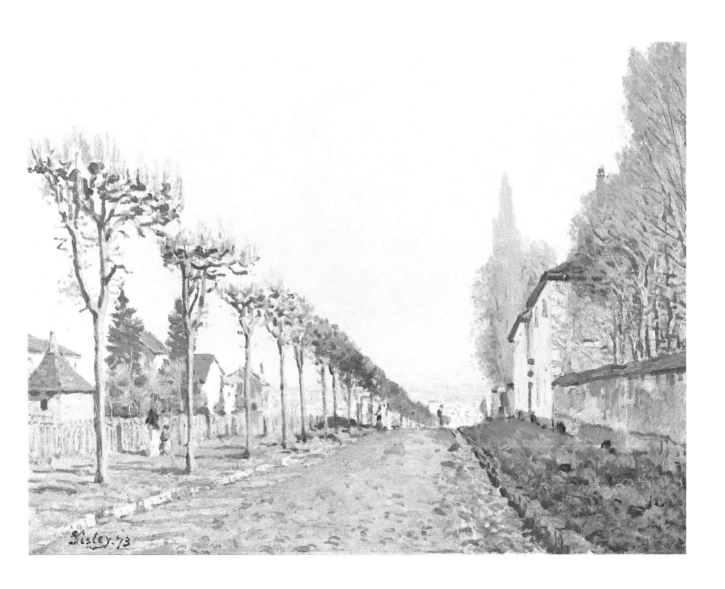

THE CHURCH AT MORET AFTER THE RAIN, 1894 ▷
Oil on canvas, 28³/₄" x 23³/₄" (73 x 60,5cm.)
The Detroit Institute of Arts

THE CHURCH AT MORET, 1893
Oil on canvas, 25⁵/₈" x 31⁷/₈" (65 x 81 cm.)
Museum of Fine Arts, Rouen

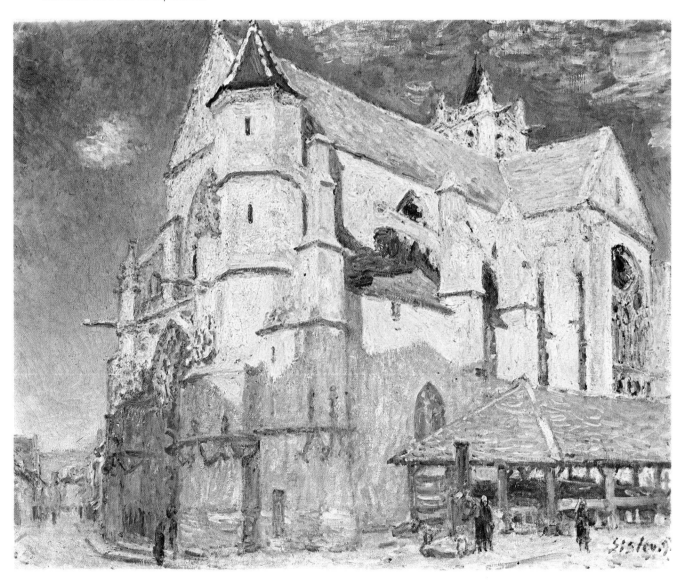

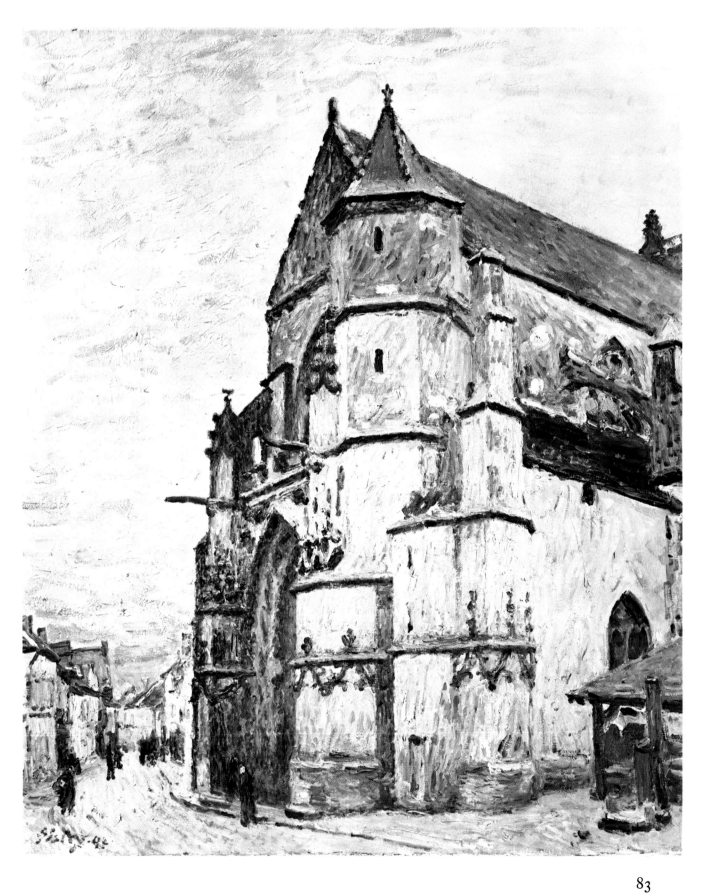

83

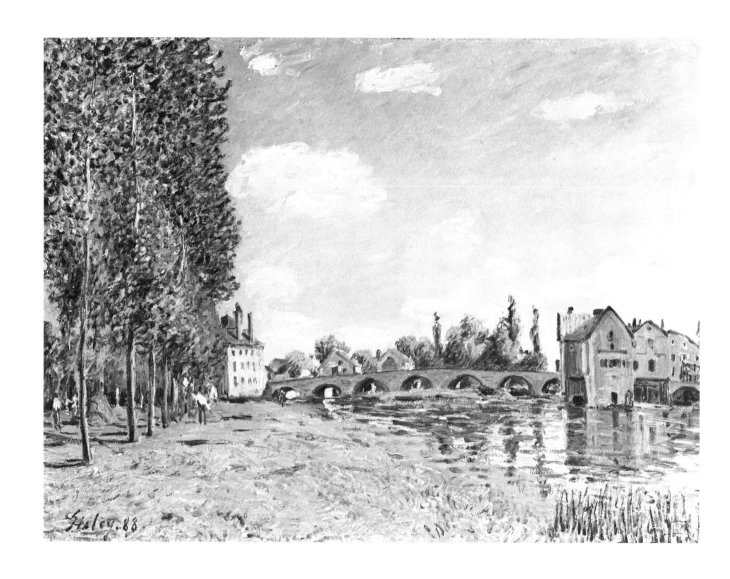

THE BRIDGE AT MORET. SUMMERTIME, 1888
Oil on canvas, $21^1/_4$" x $28^3/_4$" (55 x 73 cm.)
Collection: Acquavella Galleries, New York

church in Moret, the sparkle created by the separation of colors in small brush strokes does not destroy the walls, and the surfaces are alive without appearing fragile or unstable (see pp. 71, 84).

In addition, Sisley has a particular way of treating each of the elements in the landscape, none of which seems to him to be of minor importance. The strokes with which he paints the sky, the water, the buildings, the vegetation are not alike. He does not use the same technique to describe the various parts of a picture. There are numerous canvases in which short, separate brush strokes depict the ground or the leaves, while the sky relies on blended and transparent tones.

Sisley expressed himself clearly on this point in a letter of January 1892, written to his friend Adolphe Tavernier: « I am for a diversity of techniques in the same picture. Objects must be rendered so as to indicate their individual textures; in addition, and above all, they must be enveloped in light, as they are in nature ». All the lessons to be derived from Sisley's art are summarized in those few lines, which demonstrate to what extent the artist was clear-thinking and fully conscious of what he wanted to achieve.

Thus Sisley created for himself a pictorial vocabulary. Thanks to the variety in his repertory of methods, no picture, even on the simplest subject, is ever monotonous, and each can be studied over and over, as one repeatadly reads a passage the better to absorb the sense of each word. As one in the course of time discovers the varied meanings of the language Sisley is using, one comes to understand that he can treat the same themes over and over again without repeating himself, for, not content to note only visual impressions, he succeeds in expressing physical sensations as well: the sensation of cold and of silence in his snowy landscapes, the sensation of dampness in his Moret landscapes, the sensation of heat in the fields of Sablons or Saint-Mammès (see pp. 86, 87).

It is essential to note that these variations in technique in no way detract from the unity of the picture as a whole. Sisley uses different « words » according to the character and the nature of each element in his compositions. But these « words » result in a « sentence » which establishes their relationship and expresses their total meaning. The artist never seems to start with any initial prejudice nor does he surrender his integrity by manufacturing artificial or counterfeit products.

Early on Sisley mastered his technique, and from 1870 on (remember that his first known paintings are dated 1865) he was interested in depicting the shimmering of water by small, separate brush strokes. Even in these first paintings where Corot's influence is clearly noticeable, Sisley decided to vary his pictorial effects. The trees of this period are supple, they have a cottony softness which in no uncertain manner differentiates them from the more solid structures in the village streets. Therefore he had no need to adapt himself to Impressionism, to accept the concept of its exponents, its principles and its techniques. He himself was already such a complete Impressionist that, protected by the strength of his convictions, he was able to escape the influence of the other movements of the time.

He did not fall under the spell of the Far East, so much in vogue during that

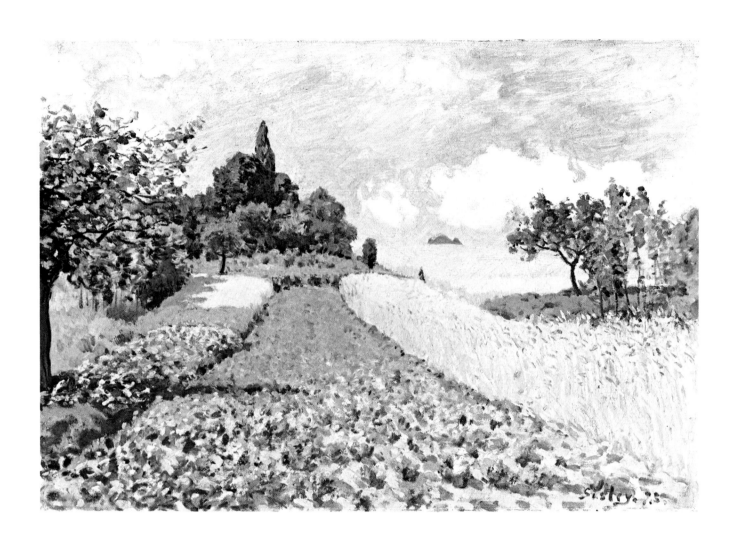

WHEATFIELDS, NEAR ARGENTEUIL, 1873
Oil on canvas, 19⁷/₈" x 28³/₄" (50 x 73 cm.)
Hamburger Kunsthalle

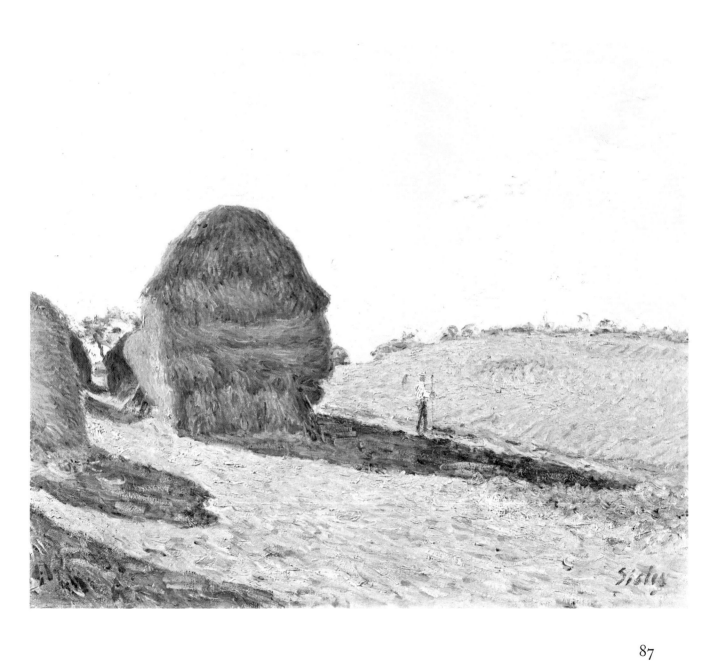

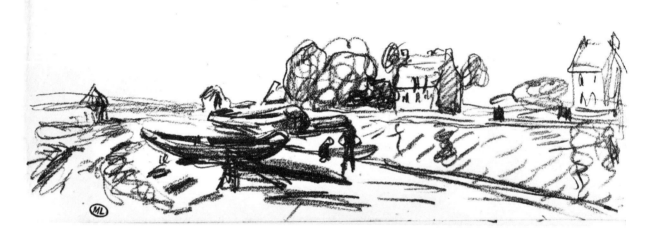

St. Mammès (The Canal Side), 1838-1885.
(From the Book of Drawings - Folio 56) 4³/₄" x 7¹/₂" (19 x 12 cm.) Louvre Museum, Paris

period, especially after the Japanese pavilion created a sensation at the 1867 Exhibition. During the following years many artists displayed a lively interest in the East: Monet and Renoir, Van Gogh, Gauguin and Lautrec among them.

Neither was Sisley attracted by Symbolism and the illusion that it was possible to introduce literary elements into painting, nor by Pointillism and the mechanical character of its scientific procedures.

His foreign travel did not seem to bring him new inspiration. His stays in England did not noticeably modify his way of looking at the world and at art, except on the occasion of his last visit, in 1897, when he discovered expanding, absolute space. He did not go to Italy, perhaps because he lacked the financial resources, but perhaps because he did not truly have the desire to visit it. In any case, the other Impressionist painters managed to travel a great deal more than he, although they too were without funds.

It would seem that Sisley possessed such an instinctive love of independence that he even refused to learn from the examples handed down from past centuries. We must keep in mind the comparisons made with Corot, Boudin and Jondkind, but these artists were practically his contemporaries and were not yet a part of the past when he started to look at their pictures.

The comparison with the Barbizon painters relies on an exclusive choice of landscape as a theme and a deep love of nature; it does not show any similarity between their technique and Sisley's. In any case, here again we have artists who can be considered contemporaries.

Sisley showed no predilection for any century other than his own. Alone among the Impressionists, he displayed no admiration for, or curiosity about the masterpieces of the past. Renoir, Manet, Cézanne, then Gauguin and Van Gogh sometimes tried to sharpen their skills by copying classical works, albeit fairly freely, or simply to get inspiration from them. Nothing of the sort existed in Sisley's case. Very early he established his own direct communication with the countryside.

RIVER BANK, no date, Pastel $11^1/_4$" x $15^3/_4$" (28,7 x 40 cm.). Private Collection

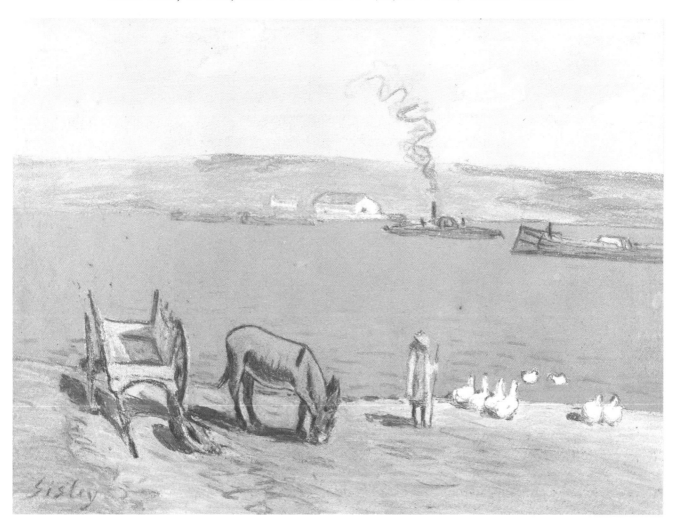

This constant rapport with nature is what is common to all of the Impressionists and forms a bond among them. It also explains the analogous techniques they employed to define and express the same perception. However, there are differences between Sisley and his comrades, which become all the more apparent when his work is compared to that of Monet and Pissarro, the two who are the closest to him.

These two painters supplement sensations or physical perception with something sensitive, almost sentimental. There is a certain affection in Monet's rendering of people. There is drama in his rivers loaded with chunks of ice, in his portrayal of disaster. There is glorified light in his Rouen cathedral. In Pissarro's landscapes, devoted to humble workers in the fields or a group of peasants in the marketplace, there is a spirit of loving brotherhood. There is an emotion in Pissarro's attitude toward daily life. But Sisley does not linger to delve into the inner meaning of things.

Monet captures what is fleeting and unstable. Sisley takes from the passing moment its enduring qualities. Monet pursues the poetic quality until his work has a certain unreality and is metamorphosed into a vision of a mirage. Sisley is aware of the poetry of nature, but receives it directly, without alteration, like an intimate friend in a real world.

Sisley is more definitive in the subjects he chooses, although he seems at least as sensitive as the others. But to express this sensitivity he is content to find comfort in the familiarity of silence and does not feel the need to use people as intermediaries.

His attitude in the presence of human figures is significant, in view of his exclusive treatment of landscapes and especially the orderly landscapes, neat and untroubled, of the Paris region. As was mentioned earlier, only one picture by Sisley portrays people: the double portrait of his children, done in 1871. One cannot really include *The Lady with a Parasol,* dated 1883, showing Madame Sisley seated in a garden in Moret, because she is only a vague form in a landscape.

This indifference to human figure is constantly affirmed. When a passerby is seen in a particular location, he is viewed only as an accessory and not as a distinct individual: a mere silhouette, or a simple stroke of the brush to add a color accent; at the most an anonymous object, similar to the dark shadow of a cypress in a Tuscany landscape, albeit less important and occupying less space. For Sisley the tree, even when seen from afar, counts much more than the man.

One does not find in his art the rumblings of the crowd, swarming like a beehive such as one sees in Paris scenes by Renoir or Pissarro which are viewed in depth, neither does Sisley depict homely family scenes such as abound in the work of the others.

Sisley's world is alive and animated, but animated by the rhythm of the passing of days and not by human gestures and attitudes. His village streets are frequently deserted, which does not imply that the houses are empty, uninhabited. He makes one feel the underlying palpitation of life and not the superficial stirrings of the inhabitants.

This communion with the countryside that surrounds him is typical of all of Sisley's work and gives it a basic unity, even if, as some commentators have noted, there is an unevenness in the quality of his pictures which is easily discernible and is due to the fact that, however brilliant they are, they were done in different stages of his evolution. Although these differences were superficial and not too precise, scholars have divided Sisley's work roughly into three periods: a first very brief one, which is distinguished by the very clear influence of Corot and lasted until about 1870; the second, which dates approximately from 1870 to 1880, at the height of the Impressionist movement, and includes the most luminous and the airiest canvases, imbued with a spontaneous quality. The third period, after 1880, is the one about which one is forced to have some reservations. It coincides with the technical perfection of the artist's craft and a style which is freer but less supple, yet the intimate and sensitive quality characteristic of Sisley is not diminished (perhaps it has become automatic) and it enables him, in any and all circumstances, to portray the passing mood without freezing it in time and space.

In a great many cases these distinctions are slight and can be said to apply to the body of his work only in a very general way, so that it would be unjustified to make any rigid differentiation or to categorize his paintings too specifically.

This constancy of inspiration and technique is a hallmark of Sisley's personal artistic style and assures him a permanent place in art annals. It also limited his ability to rise above himself and prevented him from taking those bridges to the future being erected by a new generation of young painters who, toward the end of the nineteenth century, found the natural aspects of things less and less appealing.

Therefore, if most of the leading Impressionists and their immediate successors saw these new schools adopt or adapt some of their ideas and methods, Sisley remained isolated from these currents, dependent only on himself, without followers or disciples who, starting from the groundwork he had laid, could lead the way to fresh new discoveries. His work was an end in itself, and the feeling it expressed was so personal in its nature that it could only encourage imitators rather than innovators.

There is something prophetic in the art of Monet and Cézanne, a possibility of an expanding evolution which more or less consciously calls for its continuation and development by others. Sisley's art has a serenity which does not aspire to this sort of dissemination. It finds its reason for being within itself. His observation of subjects is made purely to suit his individual aims and comes close to being a meditative reverie.

It was because of this barrier of solitude that success did not come to Sisley at the same time as to the other Impressionists, yet it was precisely his unfaltering dedication to the movement in its purest form that makes him the most total and absolute exponent of both the spirit and the form of Impressionism.

RAYMOND COGNIAT

1839. October 30, Alfred Sisley is born in Paris of English parents.

1857. Sisley leaves for London to prepare himself for a career in business. He stays four years and spends much time visiting museums.

1862. In the spring he returns to Paris. His parents agree to his giving up a business career to devote himself to art. While taking art lessons from Charles Gleyre he makes the acquaintance of Monet, Renoir and Bazille.

1863. The four artists go to the forest of Fontainebleau to paint by direct observation of nature. They stay with Père Paillard in Chailly-en-Bière.

1864. Sisley moves to 31 avenue de Neuilly, near Porte Maillot.

1865. With Renoir, Monet and Bazille, he stays with Mère Anthony in Marlotte. Paintings of Celle-Saint-Cloud. Trip in a sailboat with Renoir to Le Havre.

1866. Sisley exhibits for the first time at the Salon (two landscapes). Resides on rue Moncey. Marries Marie-Eugénie Lescouezec.

1867. A stay in Honfleur with his wife and their son Pierre. Joins Renoir in Chailly-en-Bière.

1868. Resides at 9 rue de la Paix (rue de la Condamine). In the spring, revisits Chailly-en-Bière. Renoir paints a portrait of the couple there.

1869. The Salon rejects his work. Meets painters and writers at the Café Guerbois. Lives at 27 Cité des Fleurs.

1870. Shows two Paris landscapes in the Salon. The war between France and Germany scatters the group of young artists.

1871. Sisley's father dies. During the Paris Commune Sisley lives in Louveciennes, 2 rue de la Princesse, where he sees Renoir frequently.

1872. Shows four paintings at the Durand-Ruel Gallery in London after being introduced to the dealer by Monet and Pissarro. First *Floods at Port-Marly*.

1873. Monet proposes that the group hold its own show.

1874. The first Impressionist exhibition, at the Nadar Gallery, 35 boulevard des Capucines. Sisley contributes five landscapes. At the invitation of baritone Jean-Baptiste Faure, Sisley travels to England and paints landscapes of Hampton Court. In December he is part of the committee set up to liquidate the group which had organized the Impressionist exhibition.

1875. Settles in Marly-le-Roi, where he stays until 1877. On March 24, the first sale of a collection of Impressionist paintings at the Hôtel Drouot; violently hostile reactions. Sisley exhibits twenty-one paintings. They bring very low price at auction. The largest amount, 300 francs, is paid for *Lock on the Thames at Hampton Court*.

1876. In April, a second exhibition by the Impressionist group at the Durand-Ruel Gallery, 11 rue Le Peletier. Sisley shows eight pictures. A new series of *Floods at Port-Marly*. About this time the artists and writers began to gather at the Café de la Nouvelle Athènes (New Athens), Place Pigalle, which replaced the Café Guerbois as a meeting place. Sisley appears there infrequently.

1877. In April the third exhibition of the Impressionist group at 6 rue Le Peletier. Sisley exhibits seventeen canvases. In the autumn, he takes up residence in Sèvres at 7 avenue de Bellevue. Durand-Ruel is no longer able to help him by regular purchases of paintings. On Wednesdays, Sisley lunches frequently in a restaurant-bakery on the Boulevard Voltaire run by Eugène Murer, who was a great admirer of the Impressionists.

1879. In the spring, Théodore Duret publishes a brochure on the Impressionists in which Sisley is featured. In April, Hoschédé is forced to sell his art collection, which includes thirteen Sisleys. The average price: 114 francs a picture.

1879. Desperate because of his shortage of funds, Sisley again submits work to the Salon and is rejected. He takes up residence at 164 Grande Rue, also in Sèvres. A fourth Impressionist exhibition. Sisley does not participate.

1880. A fifth Impressionist exhibition. Sisley does not participate. Lives in Veneux-Nadon, where he may have moved in 1879. Durand-Ruel resumes his support.

1881. Sixth Impressionist exhibition. Sisley does not participate. Publisher Georges Charpentier sponsors a showing of fourteen Sisleys at the Gallery « La Vie Moderne » (Modern Life). In June, Sisley visits the Isle of Wight.

1882. March: seventh Impressionist exhibition, 251 rue Saint-Honoré. Sisley exhibits twenty-seven canvases. In September he settles in Moret. In November he writes Durand-Ruel that he thinks it better to organize group-showings rather than one-man shows.

1883. June: exhibition of seventy paintings by Sisley at the Durand-Ruel Gallery. In October he returns to Veneux-les-Sablons.

1885. July: exhibition of eight landscapes by Sisley at the Durand-Ruel Gallery in London. Sends paintings to Boston, Rotterdam and Berlin.

1886. Eighth and last Impressionist exhibition. Sisley does not participate. In April and May, Durand-Ruel sends paintings by Sisley to be shown in two exhibitions in New York and decides to open a gallery in that city the following year.

1887. May: Sisley participates in the second international exhibition at the Georges Petit Gallery.

1888. June: Durand-Ruel has a show of works by Renoir, Pissarro and Sisley. The latter is featured with seventeen canvases. Sisley considers becoming a French citizen, then, in view of his financial difficulties, gives up the idea.

1889. February - March: Sisley's first one-man show in New York (Durand-Ruel); twenty-eight paintings. In November, Sisley leaves les Sablons to take up residence in Moret, rue de l'Eglise.

1890. February: painter Albert Roll has Sisley admitted as an associate member into the newly formed « Société nationale des Beaux-Arts. »

1891. March: Durand-Ruel exhibits in Boston the work of Monet, Pissarro and Sisley. Sisley exhibits in the Salon of the « Société nationale des Beaux-Arts. »

1892. Sisley exhibits in the Salon of the « Société nationale des Beaux-Arts. » His paintings are adversely criticized by Octave Mirbeau in « Le Figaro. »

1893. March: exhibition at Boussod and Valadon's, which Tavernier reviews in a long article in « L'Art Français. » In April and May, Sisley exhibits in the Salon of the « Société nationale des Beaux-Arts. » He paints several canvases on the theme *The Church at Moret.*

1894. Sisley shows eight paintings at the « Société nationale des Beaux-Arts. » In the summer he stays in Rouen, first at the Hôtel du Dauphin et d'Espagne, run by Murer, then at the home of an industrialist and art collector, François Despeaux. He brings back at least seven paintings. He moves to rue du Château, also in Moret. Again takes up the theme of *The Church at Moret.*

1895. Exhibits eight paintings (several landscapes of Normandy) at the Salon of the « Société nationale des Beaux-Arts. »

1896. May: exhibits at Murer's, in Rouen, with Monet, Pissarro, Renoir and Guillaumin.

1897. February: a major retrospective show at Georges Petit's. One hundred and forty-six paintings and six pastel drawings. In May, a four-month visit to England: London, then Falmouth (Cornwall) and Penarth (Wales).

1898. Exhibits at the Salon of the « Société nationale des Beaux-Arts. » Again considers taking French citizenship. October 8: his wife dies.

1899. January 19: Sisley dies. In February, the Bernheim-Jeune Gallery exhibits fourteen paintings by Sisley, all produced in 1897. February and March, exhibition of twenty-eight canvases at Durand-Ruel's in New York. In May, at Georges Petit's, a sale of twenty-seven paintings for the benefit of Sisley's two children.

1900. Auction sale of the Adolpe Tavernier collection at the Hôtel Drouot. Count Isaac de Camondo buys *Floods at Port-Marly* for forty-three thousand francs.

BIBLIOGRAPHY

All the volumes on Impressionism give Sisley an important place in the movement. It is impossible to list all of them here. François Daulte, at the end of his catalogue, gives good selective lists of these books and articles as well as a list of the principal documentary sources.

Works devoted entirely to Sisley are few in number; there are many more on the other Impressionist artists. Perhaps because Sisley's life was without dramatic incidents, it does not lend itself to discussion or dramatic treatment and does not offer a romantic framework of the sort that contributes so much to a lively biography. We shall therefore only list these few works:

GEFFROY, G.: *Sisley,* collection « Les Cahiers d'Aujourd'hui », Paris, Crès, 1923, 23 pl., and Paris, 1927, 60 pl.

BESSON, G.: *Sisley,* collection « Les Maîtres ». Paris Braun, n.d., 60 pl.

COLOMBIER, P. du: *Sisley au musée du Louvre.* Paris-Brussels, Marion, 1947, 10 pl.

JEDLICKA, G.: *Sisley.* Bern, Scherz, 1949; Milan, Martello, 1950; Lausanne, Marguerat, 1950, 52 pl.

DAULTE, F.: *Alfred Sisley, catalogue raisonné* of the oils. Paris, Durand-Ruel, 1959, 884 paintings reproduced.

DAULTE, F.: *Sisley, Paysages,* collection « Rythmes et couleurs ». Paris, Bibliothèques des Arts, 1961, 28 pl.

ROGER-MARX, Cl. and MURA, A.M.: *Sisley,* collection « Grands Peintres ». Milan, Fabbri and Paris, Hachette, 1966.

DAULTE, F.: *Sisley,* collection « Les Impressionnistes ». Milan, Fabbri, 1972, 204 pl.

We wish to thank the owners of the pictures by Alfred Sisley which are reproduced in this work:

MUSEUMS

DENMARK

Museum Ordrupgaard, Copenhagen
Ny Carlsberg Glyptotek, Copenhagen

FEDERAL REPUBLIC OF GERMANY

Wallraf-Richartz Museum und Museum Ludwig,
   Cologne
Staedelsches Kunstinstitut, Frankfurt
Hamburger Kunsthalle, Hamburg

FRANCE

Grenoble Museum
Fabre Museum, Montpellier
Bibliothèque de l'Institut d'Art et d'Archéologie,
   Paris
Bibliothèque Nationale, Cabinet des Estampes,
   Paris
Jeu de Paume Museum, Paris
Museum of the Petit-Palais, Paris
Museum of Fine Arts, Rouen

NETHERLANDS

Museum Boymans van Beuningen, Rotterdam

SWITZERLAND

Kunstmuseum, Bern
Kunstverein, Winterthur

UNITED KINGDOM

Tate Gallery, London

U.S.A.

Baltimore Museum of Art, Baltimore
Museum of Fine Arts, Boston
Albright-Knox Art Gallery, Buffalo
The Art Institute, Chicago
The Detroit Instiue of Arts, Detroit
The Metropolitan Museum of Art, New York
The Toledo Museum of Art, Toledo
Corcoran Gallery of Art, Washington
The National Gallery, Washington
The Phillips Collection, Washington
Sterling and Francine Clark Art Institute,
   Williamstown
Yale University Art Gallery

ART GALLERIES

Acquavella Galleries, New York - David Findlay
Galleries, New York - Schmit Gallery, Paris.

PRIVATE COLLECTIONS

Mr. and Mrs. Nicholas A. Acquavella, New York -
Nathan Cummings, New York - Oskar Reinhardt,
Winterthur.

ILLUSTRATIONS